WOOF!

Here's my "Bear" playing in the snow.

WOOF!

"We've Got Something To Tell You"

REAL LESSONS FROM REAL DOGS

By

Jasper, Buddy, Bear, Kalib, Aster, Kizzy
Cocco, Shasha, Spanky, Skipper & Olive

With the help of

Bill Lynch

Published By
Best Friend Marketing, LLC

WOOF!
"We've Got Something To Tell You"
Real Lesssons From Real Dogs

© 2012 By Bill Lynch
© 2012 Illustrations By Finn Tornquist

ISBN-13: 978-0-9839362-0-6

Published by: Best Friend Marketing, LLC
E-mail: bfk9@optonline.net
www.TheUltimateLeash.com

Book Design and Production: TeleSet, Inc,. Hillsborough, NJ

PRINTED IN THE UNITED STATES OF AMERICA

To the 37 Port Authority Police Officers
and Police K-9 Sirius,
who gave their lives at the
World Trade Center on 9-11-01.

All of them were my friends,
and I miss them dearly.
Please never forget this act of
terriorism and murder.

God Bless America.

WOOF!

Note from the Author.

Spay and neutering recommendation.

Dog ownership is both a responsibility and a blessing.

Unless you intend to breed your dog, I highly recommend

that they be spayed or neutered.

Female dogs can be an aggravation during their time in heat,

and there are health benefits to male dogs that are neutered

such as tesicle cancer prevention.

Contents

Acknowledgements

I have to mention a few people that have had a major impact on me. First, is my wife Debbie. She stood by me during those years as a K-9 Handler, when I would be called out in the middle of the night, or when I wouldn't come home because of my work. Debbie is the love of my life and I am so thankful that God granted her to me.

These next men are my mentors, who are legends in the Police K-9 world.

Jack Appalonia, a retired Police K-9 Trainer from the Philadelphia Police Department. Jack conducted my Basic K-9 Training Program, as well as in-service training for eight years.

And to Dennis McSweeny, retired Police K-9 Trainer from the Atlantic City Police Department. Dennis conducted my scent detection training (narcotic) as well as in-service training for six years.

Both of these men are nationally recognized as being the best in the business, and greatly contributed to me becoming a dog trainer.

Thank you all.

Bill Lynch, February 2012

Foreword

W ell here it is. Finally, after years of collaboration with many dogs, this book is finished. Having been involved with dogs on a professional basis since 1984, I figured it might be a good idea to put a few things on paper and give you a different perspective to understanding your dog.

You are going to learn about your dog and how to train it by hearing it right out of a dog's mouth. You see, what better way to understand the mind of your dog, than from hearing it from a dog and hopefully you will look at things from their point of view.

Please don't mind the occasional grammar issues. No one ever sent dogs to school to learn about that kind of stuff. Dog's are an instinctual bunch of characters not intellectuals. That's right — dog's have inherent characteristics. They have basic instincts. We as owners are the ones who have to understand what we are dealing with, and want to train them. You will find more about that later on. Training a dog can be an easy process if you understand the basics and how to understand your dog.

The problem is, unless you know what your dog is thinking, you will have a difficult time conveying information to them. Read on and look at things from your dog's perspective. Make this a fun experience and most of all make your dog's training experience a fun time for it and you.

Oh, one other thing. Anyone who knows the author of this book knows me to be a straight shooter who doesn't mince words when he wants to explain something. *I do not take the "Politically Correct" approach* and I don't worry about hurting feelings if I have to get a point across, especially when it comes to dogs that are in bad situations. You see, one of the reasons for this book is to protect dogs whenever possible.

As a dog trainer and someone who is around thousands of dog owners, I find that many people simply don't want to understand their dog. They can't or don't want to see what the dog is telling them in its behavior. I'm going to make a case for hearing it right out of the dog's mouth. Hopefully this approach will make more sense to you. If you have to hear the hard reality of what you might be doing wrong, then so be it. If you are one of the 95% of good dog owners then you will look at this writing as a breath of fresh air. You will learn some things you never knew. If you are in the 5% of bad dog owners, I don't really care if your feelings get hurt. I hope you wake up and smell the roses. The rest of you are a great bunch of people and I honor the fact that we can spend some time with you. This book will be speaking to the choir for some of you. I hope that you will be able to take something positive away from your reading. If you do feel outmatched with your dog, then admit it and do something about it. Take heart in what you read and apply it. In reality, training a dog is not that difficult, if you understand the whole process.

There will be times when you will read something and say to yourself, "Self, I remember reading that before. Is the guy that wrote this an idiot for saying it again?" Well the answer is no. You see I'm the guy that's heard it all and seen it all. The important thing is that the important stuff sinks in to the brains of those that need it most. OK, the smart dog owners will get this, the less fortunate whose dogs would consider their owners weird, will not. Remember, the dog is not the problem — you are.

You will also see words in *Italics*. Again, for those out there whose dogs think they are weird; *Italics* are words that are on a slight slant. Pay attention to this because it is important information to remember.

This book has a couple purposes: 1). We want to turn a poor dog owner into a good dog owner who is the Master of their beloved pet, and 2). We want to turn the good dog owner who wants better control of their dog to become the Ultimate Master of their pet. A dog needs a leader. When your dog has a leader, both of you will be happier.

CHAPTER 1

My Name Is Jasper

L et me explain who I am and where I'm coming from. My name is **Jasper**. I am a German Shepherd/Retriever mix. I am better known as a "Mutt" or "High Bred." I'm not ashamed of being a mutt because in my lifetime, I participated in some pretty incredible events. Millions of other dogs wished they could have had a life like mine. My life started out in Central New Jersey, being adopted by a very loving family. I think it was in the fall and the lady of the house saw some puppies on the back of a parked pickup truck. Because of my good looks, she immediately fell in love with the adorable puppy (me) and took me home. Well the kids and I got along great. The only problem was that I was getting bigger, (sound familiar) and the house wasn't. It was hard for me to stay in the household. Eventually, someone had to go, and believe it or not, it wasn't going to be one of the kids.

Mom, who I knew her as, called a Police Department who was looking for folks to donate dogs that resembled a German Shepherd. It wasn't that I was unwanted, but the situation did not call for me to be there any longer.

Off I went to this strange place in the middle of a big city. What a shock for a country mutt like me. I was 11 months when I finally met the new recruit who would become my partner. Oh, might I add that I had been in a four foot by ten foot kennel for two months prior to that. (A mutt can get pretty ornery in solitary for that period of time.)

Well, the first encounter with the new recruit did not go as expected, at least for him. His name was Police Officer Bill Lynch. I can remember that day. He was a big guy, who thought he knew what he was doing. You see he had pets most of his life, so he thought he was an expert. Nothing could be further from the truth! I thought that I would make a lasting impression on this poor guy. I was barking and running around in circles, but no, he didn't get the hint. I was mad for being there in the first place, and guess what? When he opened the kennel door, I gave him an unexpected welcome with my four canines on his arm. It really wasn't a big deal, because at the time I didn't know how to bite very well. (I learned how to do that the right way later on in the training.) The lesson to be learned was that Bill didn't understand the situation, and I really think that the trainers knew that, and to get a laugh, they let poor old Bill become the next victim. The trainers not only got a good laugh, but they also taught him an important lesson. He just didn't understand the situation I was in. But, don't worry; Bill was not the only one to get the same welcome by their future partners. Unfortunately, some of the guys quit on the spot as soon as they saw those four canines. (It didn't even get to the point where they were bitten.) In my estimation, my new partner didn't have enough sense to see what he was in for. (Personally, I'm glad he didn't quit, because over the next 12 years we had a great career together. After several hundred arrests, 35 bite apprehensions, over a thousand of pounds of seized drugs, over a million dollars in currency seized, working undercover as a Seeing Eye Dog, and working in a bombed out building searching for survivors, I finally retired.)

After biting him, Bill brought me a handful of food, knelt in front of me and talked to me for 10 minutes gaining my confidence. He then gave me some food to eat from his hand. It worked. It was the first of many lessons, I taught, this new recruit about the nature of a dog. Unfortunately, he didn't get it for a while, but, when it finally clicked, it was magic.

In many cases, it's hard to explain to some dog owners, that dogs are not people. We do not think like people, or understand circumstances the same way as a human would. The earlier you learn that, the better off you and your dog will be. We are basically wild creatures who over thousands of years have been domesticated. Still, we have some of our basic instincts, and always will. Some of us do some things one way and others another. Let me give you an example. Hunting dogs, hunt in different ways. A hound such as a Blood Hound smells the ground to stalk their target. A gun dog such as a Springer Spaniel will scent the air to stalk their prey. Both are hunting, but doing it in different ways. And then there are sight hounds that stalk with their eyesight.

People wonder why, after getting their new Labrador Retriever puppy home, the poor little mutt is running around like crazy acting like an idiot. "OH NO WE JUST BOUGHT THE DOG FROM H@%^$!!!!" Well, whose fault is that? It certainly isn't the dog's. It's his instinct to run and chase. That little guy could run outside all day long and only get tired when it's time to sleep at night. Jack Russell Terriers, Beagles, Border Collies, Springer Spaniels, we're pretty much the same way. We have energy and to keep us cooped up in a house isn't fair.

When you are training your dog, take into consideration what their basic instincts and characteristics are. Life will be so much easier for both of you. This book is not going to be an encyclopedia on different dog breeds. It will not explain the solution to every problem. The primary purpose of this book is explain that a dog is a dog and that we cannot be made to think or act like humans. And believe it or not, we can't talk — only write.

Humanizing a dog is the worst thing you can do and the sooner you realize that the better off everyone will be.

I'm going to encourage you, if you have not already received your furry pet into your cozy domain, to first determine what you want in a pet. Then research various breeds to determine what will make the best fit for your family, and the environment that the dog will be living in. For example, don't expect to have an easy time of raising a hunting dog in a home where it will not get exercise for at least a couple hours a day. Don't make the assumption that you can change a dog's character and mold him into what you want. Sure you can correct bad behavior, but what might be bad behavior in your mind, might be a natural instinct for the dog. Research, research, research. Yeah — go back to school and do your homework.

Suppose you want to have a quiet, calm pet and you bring home a Labrador Retriever, Springer Spaniel, Beagle or Jack Russell Terrier. GOOD LUCK. You deserve what you get for not researching the critter you just brought home. Unfortunately, the dog doesn't deserve to be placed in that environment. The little fella will soon be unwanted and everyone pays for it through frustration and plenty of stress. I'm here to help out my friends and I hope you pay plenty of attention. Those dogs can be a nightmare for even the most experienced dog owner if put in the wrong environment. Also, you might bring home a cuddly puppy from the local humane society. It looks cute (like I did), and in three months, boy oh boy, you think that you have a fox in a hen house. Pillow stuffing is all over the place, floors ripped up, the carpet is in shreds. It's all because you didn't do your homework. Hey, no one likes doing homework, but for the sake of your dog and your family, it will pay off in the long run.

The main question to prospective dog owners is: are you going to do enough to keep the hound occupied with exercise and have plenty of toys available to keep it occupied regardless of the breed type? After all the damage and stress, caused by the unnecessary situation you put yourself in, it might be hard to do damage control and get rid of the hound that caused all this damage. Hey everyone in the house has become friends with it. You have one option and that is to retrain yourself and admit that you need to do some serious training with the dog. Don't forget that your kids will become very attached to their pet and it will be a fight to get rid of the poor little "darling from h@#%." I'm going to recommend that you cut your losses as soon as possible in a bad situation like that. If you have an out of control situation, don't read a book on working out your problem. Hire a professional trainer. We will discuss what to look for in a trainer later.

You do not want to train your dog with your emotions running on high octane. At this stage of the game you need a good dose of "common sense." Unfortunately, "common sense" should be called "rare sense" when solving problems with your four-legged friend. After training hundreds of dogs for over 20 years, "common sense" is not all that common with many dog owners. The first thing Bill tells his clients during the first lesson is to remove your heart from the training process and use your brain.

Let me get back to the background of PO Bill and me. We continued our training for 16 weeks, learning basic and advanced obedience, tracking, search and rescue, criminal apprehension, search and seizure, building searches and a lot of other stuff. (After a couple of years of working together, we learned how to do drug searches.) We learned how to work in all types of environments. (Since we were going to work in a large city, our training took us to venues that even most Police K-9 never enter into.) It was early in training when I realized that I was very afraid of buses. (I hated traffic. What in the world is this gigantic beast moving so fast for, blowing black smoke at me from the side?) I got a quick dose of reality when the trainers had us walking down the middle of 42nd. Street in New York City, with traffic on both sides during the 4:30pm rush hour. Yeah, I was a "scared puppy dog," but it made me a better Police K-9. I learned not to be afraid of that environmental situation and it really wasn't as bad as it seemed. I also think Bill felt better for the experience. As a side note, I didn't even know how to climb stairs in the Academy. Bill taught me how, and it wasn't a pleasant experience. The trainer told him to pull me up the stairs then down the stairs. Then he would pull me up the stairs and then down the stairs. I became a fast learner at something I didn't want to do. That brings me to another point. The fastest way to train your dog is not to negotiate the matter. You're the boss and we're the one's working for you, don't try and coax me into something by explaining it. You have to show us what to do. That's right I said we are working for you. In reality, we dogs are at your service and we have to learn to obey whether we like it or not.

Unfortunately, most of you don't have a clue about how to train a dog, nor do you realize that you have to become our leader. The earlier that you establish in your dog's mind, that you will be the boss, the easier the training process will be. CASE CLOSED!!!

If you ever have the opportunity, watch one of those animal documentaries about pack animals such as lion, tigers or especially wolves. The leader or "alpha" animal in the pack dominates the others. That is your job. *You must become the alpha leader of your little pack.* Remember that your dog must be at the bottom rung of the metaphoric family ladder. That doesn't mean that training will be abusive. That is never acceptable. We will show you what to do. Also, you must show the rest of the family, (kids included), that they must always have control of all situations with their pet. That might be hard with young kids, but it is your responsibility to train the four-legged kid (dog) that it is below the two-legged kids on this ladder.

An Important Point To Think About

It can't be said enough that too many people think they know everything there is to know about dogs. The author of this book has handled Police K-9 dogs for over 26,000 hours and trained almost 1,000 dogs in his career. That seems like a pretty good resume. The interesting thing is that he is still willing to learn something new and is always willing to at least listen to someone who has a different training method. That's not to say he will change his training style, but might just pick up a little tidbit from someone who is also experienced in dog training. Another interesting thing is that there are dog owners whose dogs are unruly. They will tell Bill that they know better than he does and that they just have a crazy dog. To them, he only states in a firm way that you just explained why your dog is acting the way it is. (The owner was not teachable and thus, the problem is not the dog but the owner.)

A friend of Bill's who was a fighter pilot and airline pilot had over 32,000 flying hours. They were flying a "cross country" flight one day when Bill asked

Jerry if he thought he knew just about everything there was to know about flying. Jerry in the simplest of terms said, "When I feel that I have learned everything there is to know about flying, I'm going to give it up and take up sailing." Bill learned a lot from that man and fellow pilot. Jerry is a very wise person. *We hope you become wise with your dog and continue to learn and make your lifetime with your dog a continuous learning experience for both of you.*

The Cast Of Characters

The basics of understanding a dog is quite simple. Understand what your dog is telling you!!! Let me first introduce the rest of the cast of characters that will be training you.

Kalib, is a Rottweiler who at nine months weighed 90 pounds. Kalib was high energy in the house and didn't like to be walked on a leash. He would rather walk his masters, AJ and Angie, instead of them walking him. That is how it went until Bill trained A.J. and Angie. Kalib is a perfect gentleman now. Notice that AJ and Angie were the ones who were trained.

Aster is a Boxer and was two years old when he was trained. Aster's mom, Jennifer, was expecting a child, so dad, Christian, decided that it would be good for Aster to learn some manners around the house. Jennifer and Christian also learned how to bring a new baby into a home with a dog. You will learn that later in the book.

Kizzy is a Mastiff and at six months weights 90 pounds. It was smart for Henry, Mary Anne and Henry Jr. to train that monster at an early age. Boy, did he learn well from his masters.

Cocco is a Chocolate Labrador (Lab). Mike and Lee called when Cocco was four months old after Lee said to Mike "it's either me or the dog." Mike and Lee did a great job and now have an extremely manageable hound around the house.

Shasha is a "Chocolate Lab from "H _ _ _!" At six months Shasha was running wild and uncontrollable. Joan, Shashas mom, trained her so well; that on the last lesson Shasha was walking off leash.

Bear was a Golden Retriever that Bill thought was good from the beginning. Jeannie and Russ continued to do a great job and have been training him for five years now. That's right, training your dog never stops.

Spanky was probable the most hyperactive and uncontrollable Jack Russell Terrier on God's green earth. Fortunately, Spanky was trained by one of Bills mentors, Jack A. (who we referred to as "Apples"). Jack was a retired Police K-9 Trainer from Philadelphia. Jack and Bill taught Spanky, how to do prisoner apprehension just as a Police K-9 would. It's quite a sight to see.

Skipper, is a true Heinz 57. He's got a little of everything in him. Skipper's mom and dad, Finn and Gail, have done an incredible job with him. They never had a dog before and trained him with no references on how to do it. This situation is rare. Skipper was exceptional and was very comical with his reactions whenever Finn said a planned word.

Olive, is a Pekinese/Poodle mix, and at 12 pounds is a ball of fire. Olive's mom, Debbie, was the most caring and understanding dog owner Bill knew. You see Debbie is married to Bill. Believe it or not, Olive would rule the house with us. She really kept us in line. (K-9's Jasper and Buddy — Buddy would become Bill's K-9 partner after Jasper retired.)

Buddy, was Bill's second partner. Every day seemed like it was his first day of training. Buddy was worth having because of his energy level. He was the consummate working police dog and could go all day doing search after search for drugs and being happy with a play towel when he made a drug find. He was hard to keep in the house so he preferred to be kenneled outside year round. He liked it better that way.

Buddy, is a Black Lab and owned by Dave. Believe it or not, Dave had Buddy doing hand commands in the 3rd lesson.

Then there is me, **Jasper**, who went to where all the dogs go when life comes to an end. We will talk about that in the final pages of this book.

———————

CHAPTER 2

The Right Dog For Your Family

S panky talking: You don't know how often dog trainers get calls from people that have no idea what kind of mess they have gotten themselves into. Unfortunately, most people do not research the breed of dog that they brought home. Take me for example, I'm a Jack Russell Terrier. The last word Terrier would better be described as "Terrorist." Yeah we're pint sized and awfully cute, but when we get to your home, you better have plenty of patience for at least 10 years. Not all of us are like "Eddie," the star of the TV series "Fraiser." You see we were meant to dig and burrow for varmints. We're an extremely active breed that doesn't know what the word slow is until about 9:00 pm when it's time to sleep. We are non-stop — all day. There are not many people that can handle a dog like us.

When thinking about a dog, don't go off half-cocked and pick the first cute one you see. Take a look at the following check list when looking to bring a dog into your home.

First: We recommend that you determine what the purpose of the dog will be in the house. Companion, protection, therapy, hunting etc.

Second: Are there any kids in the house? What is their responsibility going to be? Oh by the way mom and dad, unless you write a contract with your kids on the first day, don't expect the little ones to pay much attention to the work and upkeep of the dog. After a couple of weeks the novelty will simply wear off. We guarantee it.

Third: Is your house big enough for the dog you want? Remember Jasper's story?

Forth: Are you willing to make the time commitment required to train the dog properly? You see, if you don't train the beast when it's a puppy, and it gets into all kind of havoc when it gets older, whose fault is it? Certainly it's not the dog's fault. You just didn't do your job. Remember, common sense is the most overlooked part of dog ownership.

Fifth: Does everyone in the family have the patience for the dog, especially if it's untrained and going bonkers on you? Just because dad wants a Lab doesn't mean that the rest of the family wants the hound in the house. Nor does it mean that it's the right dog for the household.

Sixth: Have you done your homework on which breed to select and did you find the right breeder?

Seventh: Does everyone in the household want a dog? Sometimes the husband wants a dog and the wife knows that she's going to have to clean up after it. Hey, admit is guys, you don't always think with the full perspective of what the future holds.

Eighth: Make sure that the puppy spends at least eight weeks with the litter. A well-developed dog will socialize and learn from its mother during weeks one to four. Weeks five to eight, it will learn to socialize and learn how to get along with other puppies, its littermates. Weeks nine to12 the dog should be learning how to socialize with humans.

The best way, when determining what type of dog to get, is to look through a dog encyclopedia to find which breed will adapt best to your household. Things to consider are: What is it bred for? Does it shed? How trainable is the breed? How much grooming does it need? How friendly is the breed to kids? How much exercise is required? How much of a time commitment are you willing to put into it? Etc. and etc.?

Don't consider yourself to be an expert on dogs just because you had one as a kid. It takes time and commitment to own a dog: and the time invested should start before you get the dog by doing your due diligence and researching what you are getting to.

Selecting Your Dog

"Some decisions will give you joy or
heartache for a lifetime"

— Unknown Author

Hey folks this is still **Spanky.** Yeah, the Jack Russell Terrier, better known as a Jack Russell Parsons Terrier. That's because a guy named Parson Jack Russell in England a long time ago decided to breed us for a special purpose. He wanted a high-energy dog to chase and kill badgers. They were tearing up the landscape, eating the crops and destroying everything in sight. A solution was sought, and he took several groups of terriers and created us. This is much like the way all breeds were developed. All of us originated from wolves or jackals, and over several thousand years have been domesticated.

My owner is Jack. Jack is a person that a lot of Police K-9 Handlers say, "He wrote the book on dog training." You see he is the master of trainers and has never had a dog he couldn't train. Well someone gave me to Jack as a puppy. Jack knew I would be a hand full but until you experience our personality on a personal level, you don't know what you're in for. I became the mascot for a Police K-9 unit. They tried their best to train me but, putting it in the best of terms, I overheard one handler say that it took three years for me to get through a six month program and then I still finished at the bottom of the class. If these professionals had a difficult time with me how is the non-professional going to work out.

I know we look quite cute and have great personalities, ***BUT*** we are not for everyone. Speaking in practical terms, we are *not the breed* for 99% of the population.

What I'm trying to say is, check out the breed of dog you want and desire. Some dogs are meant to hold and cuddle such as a Yorkie. Some are hunters, like me or a Springer Spaniel. Some are to guard like German Shepherds. While others don't care what their purpose is. They just want to be dogs. Some dogs want to herd. Dogs come in all different variations and you should consider the important question we discussed earlier before making your choice.

Every dog has a different personality. Let's say you have a Golden Retriever which could do no wrong. Unfortunately, it passes on and at some point you want another Golden. Don't expect the second one to be anything like the first one in personality. Any good trainer will tell you that this is a common response from owners that replace their pets with the same breed. The second or third dog is never the same as the first. Keep in mind, that if you get proper training for the dog at an early age, you can cut your aggravation by 90%. Anyone can train any pet to be obedient. That is if you work at it with a professional and start at an early age (three months). *(See Chapter Seven on Selecting A Trainer.)*

Here's another thing for the guys to think about. There have been many instances where the husband has to have a manly "Macho Dog." Recently, I heard of a husband that wanted an English Mastiff. English Mastiffs are great dogs and they are very manly, but they are also probably the biggest dogs on the planet. (He never had that large of a dog before.) The wife had some concerns that she expressed, (like hey bud, I do the house cleaning,) but no, the husband had to get his Mastiff. Well, for a few months things were going well. Then, when the dog was six months old and weighed 110 pounds, it appeared to him that, maybe his wife was right. Well, he couldn't admit it at the time, but when the dog was a year old and weighed 215 pounds, things were not as expected. You see, when a full grown Mastiff lays on the floor and stretches out, it takes up almost eight feet of space, and you need a step ladder to walk over it. The food bill was more than expected. One-hundred pounds of food adds up pretty quick. That's about 14 cups of food each day. Then when the hound had to take a dump, he never realized that the pile would be the size of a Volkswagen. A shopping bag could barely fit it all. And don't forget about the drool. Sometimes a Mastiff looks like he just swallowed a sneaker and the laces are hanging two feet out of our mouth. That's why our owners have to carry a towel with them to keep wiping our mouths. Finally after a year the "numb nut" says, "Well honey, I think we might have made a mistake." His wife quickly reminded him that "WE" is not part of the equation. This dog was going to be around the house for quite a while — so again, research what requirements you have for a dog.

Some More Things To Consider Before Getting A Dog

This might sound redundant to what you read earlier, but it is worth saying again because its important and we don't want you to get the dog as well as yourself into a bad situation!!!!

1). Do you have children?

2). What type of environment do you live in? City or suburban or country? House or apartment? Small house vs. a spacious house? Big yard or small yard?

3). How much exercise will you be able to give your dog on a daily basis? Some of us need a tremendous amount of exercise. If we don't get the exercise we require then problems will definitely develop. Unfortunately, people look at these behaviors as a dog problem, when the reality is that the owner is the problem for not giving their pet enough exercise, attention or understanding the characteristics of the breed. *It's all on you.*

4). How much time will you spend with your pet after you get it home? In many instances the amount of time at the beginning of your relationship will be a lot. As time goes on it will dwindle, and guess what, we have a tendency to get into trouble when we don't get enough attention after the novelty wears off.

5). If you have kids, what will their responsibility be in this process of dog ownership? Again as time goes on and the novelty of us goes away, mom and dad are the ones left holding the bag, or as my owner would say "Bag of Fur."

Another consideration is after you decide on a breed, where will you get it from? The most reputable breeder is one that does **"Line Breeding."** This is when the mother and father are related by breed only. There is no family (blood) relationship. Care must be made when deciding the traits of each dog though. Passive, aggressive, color, temperament are some of the things that potential owners must take into consideration when selecting a dog from a litter. You might want to stay away from the last dog chosen from a litter. That is not to say that it couldn't be good, but it is always best to see how the pups react with each other.

"Cross Breeding" is when first generation dogs are mated. This is when the mother and son or father and daughter are bred. Half siblings could also be introduced. This can be tricky and breeders do this to keep the blood line. Unless done by an expert this is not recommended, and rarely is it successful.

"Out Breeding" is a way of developing a new breed of dog. Remember I said Jack Russell Terriers were bred by the Parson? Well this is becoming a trendy thing these days. Labs and Poodles become "Labadoodle," a Poodle and a Cocker Spaniel, become a "Cockerpoo." A Pug and a Beagal become a "Puggel." You know what I'm getting at. The variations could be endless. My friend Bear is a cross between a Golden Retriever and Yellow Lab. His temperament as well as appearance is second to none.

Then we have better known **"Heinz 57," "High Bred."** These guys are the result of sneaking around and getting it together. Things just happened and most time no one knows who or where the dog came from. It becomes a guessing game as to what you have. Many a great dog comes from this background. Our friend Bear is a Golden Lab but looking at his tail it appears that there is possible Akita somewhere in his line. Who cares, he's still a great dog. Skipper is a great example of a Heinz 57. He was one of the best dogs we ever knew.

For a price, usually between $100 and $200 you can have a DNA test done to determine what breeds your dog has in it. Recently we spoke to a lady that had a very handsome St. Bernard with AKC papers. She did a DNA test and found several breeds. The one breed in it that surprised her was Beagle.

If at all possible, make sure you know the mother and father of the pup you decide on. If not study the pup and look for an even-tempered dog that enjoys playing with the other dogs and not a bully type. Do not take the shy dog that is cowering in the corner just because you feel sorry for it. It's temperament could result in problems in the future.

Pet shops are not the best place to buy a dog although there are some very reputable places out there. Many times they are buying their stock from Puppy Mills that are inbreeding or "Cross Breeding" dogs for the sake of raising cash.

Breeders, for the most part, are reputable if they come with a good recommendation. They are the way to go if you want a pedigree. You might spend a bit more money but it will be worth the extra expense. If you want a pedigree and don't have the money to purchase it, you can look at adopting from an animal rescue. There are Breed Specific Rescues. As a rule, the cost of getting a dog from a rescue will be between $150-$300 for the vet expenses and shots. Rescue dogs are almost always fixed, adding to the cost. One thing to remember is that if a dog is in a rescue, it might be coming with issues. Another factor to consider is, that a rescue dog will most likely be an adult. And, don't expect to get AKC papers from a rescue although you might get lucky.

Adoption is also a good way to bring a pet into your home. Many times dogs that were trained had to be given up due to a family hardship. Dogs in shelters also might be more mature than a pup and the puppy stage will be long gone. Remember, study the dog and don't take him just because you feel sorry for it. Don't select a dog after seeing it only one time. Go back and observe it on several occasions and bring different people with you to see how he responds to everyone.

Suppose a dog is abused by a man, or a woman, or even kids, and a man is not introduced to the dog initially. When the man is finally introduced to the dog at home, problems could be waiting. The man who the dog associates with abuse could be the most well-meaning soul in the room, but the dog will only identify that a man had abused it. Just consider this because it has happened many times.

I always recommend training and with enough care and attention you will have a happy life together. In some cases, dogs from shelters can have issues. Someone gave it up for a reason. Check that out and press the folks for an answer. I heard of a situation where the shelter had a small puppy. The attendant said it was a Terrier. The folks took it home thinking it be a Boston Terrier-type dog. After it grew up, it turned out to be a Pit Bull Terrier. The dog was a good one for the family, but was not the small terrier they expected it to be.

Children's Contract To Have A Dog

Pet ownership can be a rewarding experience for children and will teach responsibility that they cannot learn anywhere else. This is an experience they will never forget. In the experience of most trainers, dogs come into a home with the understanding of the parents that each child in the home will care for their new pet. Experience indicates that this gets old after two weeks (if that long) and mom and dad are the ones stuck with the hound. I recommend that for children over nine years old (depending on their maturity), a contract be signed by the child. This offers a little more emphasis to their responsibility and requirements of pet ownership by everyone in the house. If the children fail to care for their pet then mom or dad (preferably both) can show the signed paper indicating to the child that these are the rules. I don't apologize for sounding harsh. This is an outstanding lesson for kids to learn from an early age.

We always like to emphasize that life is about personal responsibility. We as dogs need a leader and the sooner kids learn this; the better it is for everyone. To date I know of only one family that returned the dog after the kids wanted a dog and made all the promises of taking care of it. After a couple weeks they stopped taking care of the dog and dad was doing all the care. Tim didn't want the dog from the start. There were no questions and the contract was there for them to see. The kids still wanted the dog but they didn't fulfill their part of the agreement. In a situation like this, it was best for everyone involved to give up the dog. Sure the kids were sad, but they were also warned and their dog was paying the price. If one of the parents is absolutely against getting a dog, then don't get one. *(See the very last pages of this book for an official-looking, suitable for framing and hanging, contract for your child or children to sign.)*

Kids And Dogs

When it comes to kids and a dog in the house, mom and dad must realize that the dog will look at a child differently than they do an adult. The reaction will be different and it is mom and dad's responsibility to control the behavior of both the dog and the kids.

Kids have a tendency to be on the floor and play with the dog. Many adults will do the same. When this happens, the puppy will identify those that are playing with it as a littermate. That is fine up to a certain extent. When a dog identifies family members as littermates, there might be a problem, because in many situations the dog will attempt to become the "Alpha" figure in the pack. This is not a good result. Be especially careful with your kids playing with dogs. You don't want to stop it altogether but bear in mind that a little bit of control over the dog while playing with kids will work out best for the future.

Dogs understand what is called "The Pack Order." Dogs, being pack animals realize that there is an order to the hierarchy in a family or pack. Earlier, we discussed how, when you bring a dog home, you want, in a very caring way to let the dog (puppy) know that you are the leader of the pack and the dog is on the bottom rung of the metaphoric ladder. Pack mentality never leaves a dog's behavior. Many cities have problems with wild packs of dogs. These are dogs that have run away from home, have found other dogs and they form a pack. There is a leader (Alpha Dog) and then there is the follower, which is the lowest dog on the ladder. This is the natural behavior of a dog.

The best scenario is to brief the kids on how the dog will be treated when it comes home. When you bring the dog home you will walk the dog outside immediately and let it relieve itself in its special area. (We talk about this later.) Then bring the dog into the house and let it sniff around. No play time for the kids yet. After a little bit of time (½ to 1 hour) the puppy will begin to feel comfortable in its new environment. (I recommend that you have a crate before you bring the dog into your house and introduce it to the crate as soon as possible, to let it know that the crate is its bedroom.

Remember that dogs are cavernous animals and like a close surrounding when it is sleeping. It creates a safe feeling for them.) In their original habitat, wolves would find shelter under a log or in a cave. Your home is a couple steps removed from this environment and it is best to let them know that they have a safe place to go. Also, keep the dog contained to the kitchen with gates. This will be their main room for six months to a year. If an accident occurs, the clean-up will not be as bad as if it were on carpet. Clean any mess with a deodorizing cleaner that does not have ammonia in it. Again, bring the waste to an area in the backyard that you want the dog to relieve itself. The dog will smell it when you walk it there and will know that that area is ok to do its business.

Do Not Allow The Puppy To Sleep In The Bedroom!!

Dogs sleeping in a bedroom create many of the problems that dog trainers must deal with. Jealousy issues are one of the main problems and it can only get worse as time goes on. To stop a potential problem, keep the dog in a crate.

Kids love to wrestle with puppies and puppies like it also. Remember that dogs are pack animals and in the wrestling mode, dogs are sizing up each person it is with. They are determining who is the strong one, (Alpha Leader) and who is the weak one, (the follower). They are doing this by internally analyzing kids and adults by physical strength, body language and tone of voice.

Parents, please stay consistent with your children. This will teach them a lesson that will last for a life time.

After you have selected your new pet, please read this poem "A Dog's Prayer" by Beth Norman Harris and make it your commitment for the rest of your dog's life.

A Dog's Prayer

Treat me kindly, my beloved master,
For no heart in all the world, is more grateful
For the kindness, than the loving heart of mine.

Do not break my spirit with a stick,
For though I should lick your hand between the blows,
Your patience and understanding will more quickly teach me things
You would have me understand.
Speak to me often, for your voice is the world's sweetest music,
As you must know by the fierce wagging of my tail
When your footstep falls upon my waiting ear.

When it is cold and wet, please take me inside,
For I am now a domesticated animal
No longer used to the bitter elements.
And I ask no greater glory than the privilege of
sitting at your feet beneath the hearth.
Though you had no home, I would rather follow you through ice and snow
Than to rest upon the softest pillow in the warmest home in all the land,
For you are my god and I am your devoted worshiper.

Keep my pan filled with fresh water,
For although I should not reproach you were it dry,
I cannot tell you when I suffer thirst. Feed me clean food, that I may stay well

To romp and play and do your bidding, to walk by your side, and stand ready,
Willing and able to protect you with my life should your life be in danger.

And, beloved master, should the great Master see fit
to deprive me of my health or sight,
Do not turn me away from you.
Rather hold me gently in your arms
as skilled hands grant me the merciful boon
Of eternal rest — and I leave you knowing with the last breath I drew,
My fate was ever safest in your hands.

— Beth Norman Harris

CHAPTER 3

Dog Training
(An Overview)

Basic dog training is really quite simple. That is if you — *#1 Know what you're doing*, then, *#2 Know what your dog is thinking.*

Don't forget that this is coming from the perspective of dogs. I think we know more about this than the average person. I'm speaking from experience, yes this is Jasper telling you how it is. Don't think that you can humanize a situation with a dog. It just doesn't happen that way. Look at it this way. The next time you read "The Good Book" (Gods Word — *The Bible*), turn to the first page, Gen. 1:26. In that verse, you will find that God instructs *man to be the ruler over all the creatures of the earth.* Your dog is not man, but a creature. *When dealing with a problem scenario, sit back and take a look at the actions of your dog, then, do something about it. Do not act under emotions. And most importantly, realize that you are dealing with a dog.* Sorry to be so forward but you have a dog and not a person. We don't understand the way people do, don't reason the way people do and don't understand language as you folks understand a language.

Don't get into a definition war with yourself and the dog. "Sit" means "Sit," "Down" means "Down," "Stay" means "Stay," "Come" means "Come" and most importantly "No!!" mean's "No!!" This should be understood the first time you say it, not repeated over and over again. Dog's don't have a vocabulary. We respond to sounds and tones. Communication is one of the most important aspects of training. Don't compromise on issues with your furry friend. Also, don't kid yourself that you know more than you really do. Remember when Bill tried to approach me in the kennel. Well, he thought he knew how to handle the situation. Quite frankly, he was outmatched and just because he had pets all his life, it didn't mean that he knew what he was doing. There will be many situations in your home where you will be outmatched and out witted by the nature and instincts of your dog. Realize that now, and your life will be better for it.

After Bill's incident with me during our original meeting, the Sr. Trainer, Jack, who as I said before, wrote the book on Police K-9 Training, had a meeting with all the prospective handlers. The first thing he said was, "How many of you have had dogs during your life?" Everyone raised their hands. The next thing he said was, "If you want to succeed in this program, forget everything you think you know about dogs and listen with both ears and do as we say." That was a pretty hard reality when you have a group of guys that thought they knew something about dogs and especially that they were for the most part "Type A" personalities. (For those who don't know what a "Type A" personality is, you probably don't have it. Type A's are extremely motivated, don't take no for an answer, think they can control any situation, sees a problem and fixes it, and is not a person that is wondering what God placed them on earth for.) Most of the handlers listened and started their K-9 career from zero knowledge about dogs. Most of them forgot everything they thought we knew about dogs. These were the guys that excelled. So, don't feel bad when a dog tells you in their behavior that you really don't know as much about dogs as you think.

One of the most important things to remember in training your dog is to *be as consistent as possible*. Confusion is the root of all screwed up situations.

Suppose you went to work for the first time, and the most experienced person at the job told you how perform a task. It's only logical that you would follow his instructions. The next day he told you how to do the job in a different way, and the next day he told you a different way from the first two. You could not master the job because the instructions were being changed every day. The same lesson can be applied to dog training. Let's reiterate. You don't know how many people change their own commands to their pets from day to day. Boy can that be frustrating to your four-legged friend. Just think about it — one day you tell Fido to sit on command and he doesn't sit. Then you say, "sit, sit, sit," then make Fido sit. Well now Fido thinks he's supposed to sit after the third time you say it. You forgot the initial concept of sitting on command the first time, and changed it to sitting the third time you said it. Guess what, your dog is confused because you're confused. The end result is a confused dog and confused and angry owner. Whose fault is it? Yep, "YOU ARE AT FAULT."

Voice Control is another basic element of training a dog. If you are mono tone, (which means you have no pitch or tone in your voice), your dog will have a problem understanding you. You will have to learn how to raise and lower your voice tone. *Voice tones, low range, mid range and high pitch are important to get a dog to respond to you.* I can remember one handler who was mono-toned and boy was his dog ever confused. The poor dog didn't know whether he was coming or going. This is simply how it goes.

For "praise" a high-pitched voice will be used. If you are a man, temporarily become a soprano. "Good boy" or "good girl" is what you say along with hand affection. Don't worry if you get the boy or girl word wrong. We dogs can't understand words. We understand sounds and voice tone or pitch. I certainly wouldn't be offended if you said "good girl" to me, even though I am such a manly hound. The most important part of praise is the loving hand contact and a high pitch excited voice. Words used in dog training should be one syllable. *The tone of your voice and the sound coming out of your mouth is what matters.* As long as you add hand affection with your high-pitched voice praise, we will get along just fine.

For "correction," a low stern voice is used. Yes, I know ladies, this is where most of your complaints come from. We can't tell you how many times we hear, "The dog listens to my husband, but not to me." Take into consideration what we just went over. Ladies, generally speaking, unless you've been a smoker for a long time and your voice sounds like George Burns, your usual tone is high pitched. It sounds like praise to us and that is how we treat it. We keep doing what we're doing even though we're driving you nuts, not realizing that you want us to stop our bad behavior. Just imagine that Fido commits an offense in your lovely home. Being the lady of the house, you are offended and want to take action. Your first instinct is to start yelling and chasing Fido. Fido hears the yelling lady chasing him and it sounds like a "Screaming Banche" doing an Indian war dance. Fido hears a praise tone coming from the lady that is chasing him and thinks that it's playtime. The situation is exasperated by your actions. The situation would have been easily resolved if you calmly put the leash on Fido and simply corrected him in a low stern voice saying, "NO."

When you as a dog owner have a situation with your dog and it isn't going well, take a deep breath and wait a moment. Think about the situation and don't lose control. Remember; take your heart out of the equation. Take action only when you're emotions are settled. If you are in an emotional state you will lose the battle. You can take that to the bank.

A "Command Tone" is a mid-range tone that you will use when giving one of the commands: Sit, Down, Heel, Come, Stay. No raising your voice, no deepening your voice, just a normal voice that the dog hears from you all the time. Again use one-syllable words.

Body Language is a very important part of the training process. We will discuss this in further detail later. The one thing to remember is that we feel the softness or strength of a person and that tells us a lot about who you are. There are differences between men, women and kids.

In general we respond to men and women differently. As I said, ladies do have a soft touch and a soft voice. Men on the other hand have a deeper stern voice, and strong touch. *It is best for everyone who is training a dog to realize your weaknesses and strengths and adjust to make the communication process between you and your dog as smooth as possible.* Men, sometimes you don't have to be overly firm with your dog and *ladies, you can not show any weakness towards your dog.* Many times men don't realize how firm you are with your dog and it can effect the situation in a negative way. Sometimes, ladies can be soft on a dog without realizing it and the dog will take it as weakness and take advantage of the situation.

Positive Reinforcement puts the icing on the cake or as we would say, the gravy over our dog chow. Remember when you were a kid and you did something good for mom or dad, and never received recognition for the job well done. Pretty disappointing, wasn't it. Did you feel like going out and doing another good task? The answer is probably, "NO," and for good reason. "Positive reinforcement," whether received by a human or a dog, has its benefits. Suppose at your job, your boss never gives recognition. What's the end result? Yeah that's right, bad moral. You see, you can *apply positive reinforcement to almost every situation when tasks are completed properly,* so why not apply it to your dog. Yeah, the word in most packs is, "A praised dog is a happy puppy." We're not going to spend a lot of time on this subject, because it speaks for itself. Do unto your pet, as you would want someone to do unto you. (Remember this the next time your kid's do a good job. It works, and most important, your bond with them will grow.)

"Positive reinforcement" is a simple physical contact with your pet, by petting his head, scratching his back or where ever it feels best and adding a "good boy" or "good girl." This physical contact is also called "bonding." It is an important factor in the relationship between you and your pet. Believe it or not, studies have also revealed that it is also good for you to have that physical contact with us. For some people, blood pressure even drops when they have physical contact with a pet.

"Positive reinforcement" is extremely important, BUT don't over-do it. There are two types of *positive reinforcement.* One is for *bonding and one is for training.*

"Bonding Reinforcement" is a constant petting or massaging your pet. With

"bonding reinforcement" you want to gain the confidence of your dog or comfort it. Unfortunately, "bonding reinforcement" doesn't always continue as we and our owners get older. Personally, I always thought it was great when PO Bill and I got home and after dinner, he would sit on the couch and I would lie next to him. He would give me an occasional pet on my head while he was watching TV, and I knew that I was an important part of his life, even after spending eight hours at work. I also knew that he had special time with his wife and kids and that they always came first so I had to give them their distance by staying in my crate.

"Training reinforcement" is a short pat on the head. The problem we canines have is that the "bonding reinforcement" feels great, and we don't want it to stop. When we get constant "positively reinforcement" for an extended period of time during a training session it becomes "bonding reinforcement," and we have a tendency to break our commands wanting more of that physical contact. You see, most times we can't reason the different types of positive reinforcement. Get into a routine of short "positive reinforcement" (a pat on the head) for training and extended "positive bonding reinforcement" during bonding.

CHAPTER 4

Basic Obedience

I n this section you are going to learn the most basic ingredients to fulfilling your dream of having a trained dog. It is completely up to you though. You're the brains of the group or at least, it's supposed to happen that way. Unfortunately after speaking with some of the guys in the pack, we have heard of a few situations where the dog was, way, way smarter than the owner.

Ask any experienced trainer and they will concur with me. Don't get a big head about being the supposed brains of the group, although, we're not as dumb as you think either. A different dog character will handle each section of this chapter. The dog explaining a particular training tool was extremely proficient in the discipline or lack of a discipline that we will be discussing.

It will be important for you, as well as your dog, to take your time in learning this material. Assume that you and Rover are going to learn this at the same pace and for the first time. Remember, *it is extremely important that you keep your training program as simple as possible.* Dog training should be fun for everyone involved.

In another chapter, you will learn about all the various types of leashes and collars in a very detailed manner.

Basic Training Tools

Before we talk about training, we need to discuss some of the tools and elements required for the process to be successful. Some of this might sound like it is obvious, but take it from a dog with a stubborn owner, don't take anything for granted when people are involved. Many a good dog has been ruined by a knuckle headed owner that took everything for granted.

This is Tex speaking. I was a great dog but the ignorance of my owner almost ruined me until he got some understanding on what he was doing wrong. Sit back, read and absorb this information and your dog will love you to pieces for it.

COMMON SENSE: "Common sense" might not sound like a tool, but think about it. Take a look around at all the people that don't use common sense on a daily basis. It gets even worse when people use "no sense" at all, acting more like a moron, and making a situation very confusing for your dog as well as themselves. In that case — the supposed common sense should be referred to as "rare sense." "Common sense" is only a matter of looking at the big picture, possibly taking a step back and then making a decision on how you will handle a training situation with your dog. For some people, "common sense" is a split second decision. If you are wondering why I said that, then you are probably in the category of needing to work harder at using "common sense." Using "common sense" means that you will not make split second decision. So what if it might take minutes to figure out your training solution for a problem with your dog. If you are the type of person that can't take a minute to evaluate a problem with your dog, then you're probably wondering why you even got a dog in the first place.

I'm a Chocolate Labrador named **Sasha,** and I can assure you that common sense was a very important ingredient in the success of my training. My owner Joan was as conscientious as anyone could be, and is a good example for everyone to follow. Understanding a situation is the first step to solving it. Joan was the type of owner that if she did not understand something or was even unsure, she would make sure she had the correct solution prior to taking action.

I was once told by a couple of my Police K-9 buddies, that there were lapses of common sense at the academy on the part of a couple of handlers. One story was about how the trainer switched dogs in a kennel (the two dogs looked almost identical.) The handlers were into their 8th week, yeah, two months of working with the same dog everyday. The handler took the dog out and couldn't understand how the cotton-picking dog got so dumb over night. The funny thing was that he worked with an untrained dog for an hour before he figured it out. (I know, this doesn't say much about the selection process of the K-9 Unit at that time, but it has changed for the better over the years.) Unfortunately, the embarrassed compadre did not look at the total picture when he could have immediately seen that he had the wrong dog. He acted without taking a minute to see what was wrong. What might be a logical assumption on your part could turn out to be a mistake in effort and in the end result.

PRAISE (Positive Reinforcement): "Hi," I'm **Buddy,** owned by Dave. Positive reinforcement or praise is the most important factor in getting the most out of your dog. Take it from me. My owner is probably the best at giving positive reinforcement. Dave has been the most beneficial person in my life. Yeah I still need a good check (correction will be explained later) every once in a while but, because of the praise I received from him, I just wanted to please him, at least most of the time.

Praise reinforcement might not appear to be a training tool, because you think of a tool as something physical. Anything you do with your dog using your physical abilities is a tool. You are using your voice and physical reinforcement, praise, as a tool. Take athletes for example, whether they are amateur or professional, they reinforce a good play with a pat on the back or butt. They're not doing it because they want to be sweethearts. It's the positive reinforcement and receiving the recognition of doing a good job that is a great moral booster for all of us. As for a dog, we do like the way it feels. A nice pat on the head feels just great.

Praise is saying a simple phrase like "good boy" or "good girl" in a high pitch voice. The words must be accompanied with an action though. Keep the leash in your right hand so you can physically praise with your left hand. The dog should always be on your left side. The dog's right shoulder will be next to your left leg. (That is the industry standard, and will be explained later.) There is a reason for that. The left hand is for petting me. The slightest bit of hand contact means a lot and we'll do just about anything to get your positive attention. When it comes to praise, get your excitement level up. Believe it or not, we feel your excitement, and sense your pleasure for a job well done. Don't forget the difference between "bonding reinforcement" and "praise reinforcement" discussed previously.

Your voice, when giving praise must be different from correction or giving a command. It was discussed by Jasper earlier. If you're a man, you must temporarily become a soprano. Get the highest pitched sound out of that mouth and just say "good boy, or good girl."

Just speak in a high-pitched voice or whistle around a dog. You will see a different reaction by them than when you speak in a deep voice. They generally give you a tilted head, or a peculiar look towards you. Well, you just got their attention, and it was in a positive way. Apply your praise in the same manner, and you will have your dog jumping through hoops.

All we want is to make you happy. We truly want to be your Best Friend. Sometimes when we are lacking that little bit of attention that we really need, we can get a little rambunctious. Before you get mad, think about the whole situation. (Remember "common sense") We are just looking for attention. We might have a temper tantrum to get attention. Correction might be the initial solution to the bad action but the situation was probably your fault to start with. Later you will read the story about K-9 Buddy jumping into the pool, (and by the way I got a laugh or bark out of that myself when I heard about it). He told me that he was, in a way, looking for attention, but didn't know how to get it any other way. He was also tired of being cooped up so he took the liberty of stretching his legs.

Well, that pretty much takes care of giving praise or positive reinforcement to your dog. Remember one thing, don't praise your dog for being cute when in actuality they're doing something wrong. The praise for bad or cute behavior will only reinforce the behavior, and that's where small problems become big problems. Keep an open mind. We have feelings too, and need your attention. Don't just give us your attention only when we do something wrong.

Types Of Collars

Collars come in all different styles. Some are good for training and some are not. The experience of the trainer will dictate the type of collar used. We say this for a couple reasons. All dog trainers come with all varieties of training methods. Basically it is the end result that you are looking for. Your goal will be to have your dog doing perfect obedience, (off lead with hand commands in 12 weeks). That does not mean that the head halter, pinch collar or any other collar is used for the end result. If you as a dog owner use the head halter or pinch collar to control your dog, then you do not have a well-controlled dog. A controlled and obedient dog will listen while off leash and no gimmicks are needed. Any dog can be trained to be like this. It just takes patience, a little bit of know how and plenty of practice.

As we said earlier, look at what the professionals use and follow them, police K-9 units and professional breed handlers. A qualified professional dog trainer worth their salt will not use a head halter to train a dog.

The types of collars will be given a number rating on its acceptable use as a training collar. Number one being the highest and number three being the lowest level of effectiveness.

METAL CHAIN COLLAR (CHOKER) #1: The Chain Training Collar is a tool used by many trainers to get the attention of the dog being trained. THE CHOKER *IS NOT HARMFUL IF USED CORRECTLY!* The choker collar is used to get the dog's attention and to let them know that their behavior is unacceptable. We will discuss how to effectively use it in a future chapter.

Choker Chain

Looking at the illustration, you will make a backwards "P" with the chain. Having the backwards "P" in front of you, place it over the dog's head while it's on your left side. When you pull on the loose ring, it will slip loosely back and forth.

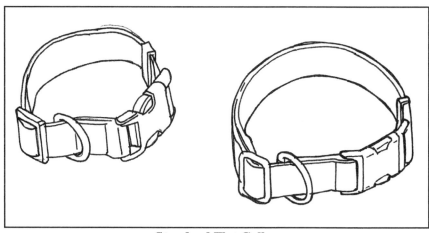

Standard Flat Collar

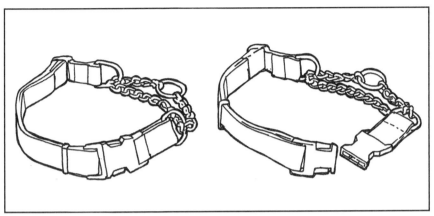

Martingale Collars

STANDARD FLAT COLLAR #3: The standard collar is made of either nylon webbing, cotton fabric or leather. This collar is least effective, because it is very soft on the dog's neck, thus you cannot get the dog's attention. These are great for dogs after they are trained.

MARTINGALE COLLAR #1: Martingale collars are becoming more and more popular. This collar combines the standard flat collar with a training "choke" collar. Martingale collars come in a couple variations. Some are available that do not have a clip. With this type, you must slide it over the head of the dog and then adjust it to the proper neck size while on the dog. To make sure it is not too tight you should be able to fit four fingers comfortably between the collar and the neck of the dog. Best Friend Marketing LLC, (www.theultimateleash.com) is now making available a Martingale collar that has a metal side release clip on it. This system makes it easier for the handler to adjust the collar while it's off the dog and when it is the proper size, just put it around the neck and secure the clip. Another type of Martingale collar is one that does not have a chain, but has fabric instead. This type of Martingale collar is for dogs that have sensitive necks such as Grey Hounds and Whippets or any dog that your vet says has a neck issue. The Martingale collars that are 100% fabric are not as effective as the Martingales with the chain. The reason is that the chain makes a reinforcing noise the dog will respond to and the chain has a very smooth release action when pulled.

The Martingale collar has several advantages over the metal training choker: 1). It can be made snug on the dog's neck so it fits securely at the top of the neck just under the jaw; 2). It can be adjusted when it is off the dog and then placed around the dog's neck then secured with the buckle; 3). It has a chain that makes a sound that the dog hears. The sound of the chain is a reinforcement that the dog hears and has respect for the potential use of a quick check (correction); and 4). The Martingale collar cannot be put on the dog's neck incorrectly like a choker. It works properly regardless how you put it on as long as you snug it up so four fingers can fit between it and the neck.

This collar can also be ordered through the Ultimate Leash website. These collars are available in matching collars to The Ultimate Leash.

PRONG COLLAR (PINCHER) #2: We in the canine world call the pinch collar a lazy persons tool to control a dog. The pincher is a collar that has prongs that protrude into the dog's fur. By pulling on the chain of the collar, the prongs tighten towards the dog's neck. Contrary to popular belief, the prongs do not dig

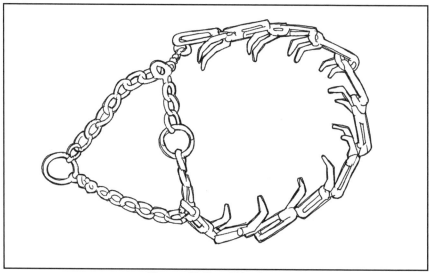

Prong Collar (Pincher)

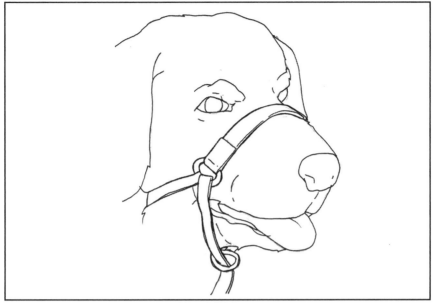

Head Halter

into the dog's neck. The dog stops pulling before it gets to that point.

The reason it's called a lazy persons tool, is because too many people start out using the prong collar before making any attempt to train their dog in a traditional manner. There are occasional times when the prong collar is effective, such as when an 80-pound lady is attempting to walk a 120-pound Rottweiler. She is out matched and needs the extra reinforcement as a safe guard.

HEAD HALTER #3 (over the nose): Dogs hate these silly things. In most cases trainers using these only indicates their lack of experience. No offense, but look at it this way, would you like to have something over your face and being pulled around? There have also been cases of neck injuries with this type of equipment. An experienced trainer does not need a gimmick like this to control a dog.

Head halters can cause neck injuries. Think about it. Suppose your dog has a head halter on and while on a walk, the dog goes in one direction and you accidentally walk the opposite way, pulling on the leash which is attached to the halter, which is attached to the dogs head. I would think that something has to give. It's not going to be the equipment. If anything is going to give, it's going to be the dog's neck. Yep, a good case of "whiplash." Just something to think about.

BODY HARNESS #3: There are many types of body harnesses. In many cases, they only encourage a dog to pull. Think about it. A sled dog uses a body harness to pull. A competition pulling-dog uses a body harness. A Police K-9 who is tracking uses a harness. This tool encourages the dog in each case to pull. The harness goes over the shoulders and distributes the pressure of the leash making it easy to pull.

There are instances where a harness might work, but that is up to the owner. There are some harnesses that are "no pull harnesses." The question is, what happens when the harness comes off? The dog resumes it's normal behavior which is usually pulling. Is this really training the dog? OR is the harness just subduing the dog while on a walk. If a dog has an issue with its neck then a harness is a good solution. However, many dog owners complain that some dogs in their own creative ways, can slip out of a harness.

ELECTRONIC COLLAR'S #1-2 (E-collars): E-collars do have a purpose, but we feel that they are very much misused. Without the proper training, even the most difficult dog will not respond in a positive manner. E-collars can be used as an abusive tool and should only be used by someone who has been trained properly.

We highly recommend E-collars for difficult situations such as excessive barking. This will not always solve the problem though. One of the K-9 unit's police dogs would bark excessively whenever in a vehicle. The higher the setting, the worse the barking became. He was actually wearing out batteries. That dog eventually was assigned to the subway system.

E-collars when used properly and with the dog that will respond positively can work wonders. Make sure you know what you are doing first. We know of many trainers and have seen the results of using E-collars and the dogs are

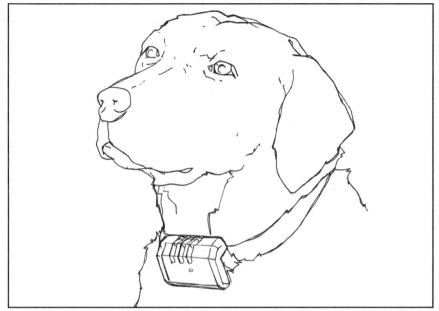

Electronic Collars (E-collars)

outstanding. Professional advice is always recommended if you are not familiar with a piece of equipment.

BARK COLLARS #1: Bark collars are a great tool for dogs that bark just for the sake of barking. These are dogs that are not communicating with other dogs, they are not alerting you of an intruder, and they are not trying to get your attention. They are just barking, just to bark. I don't know about you, but they are a major nuisance. Hey, we dogs want a little peace and quiet also and don't need an uncontrolled barking hound bothering us.

Bark collars come in different types. One type is electronic. When the dogs start to bark, the neck expands and the dog receives a negative reinforcement in the form of a small shock. The level of shock can be increased. Another form of bark collar is the citronella spray collar. When the dog start to bark, the neck expands and a citric odor is emitted from the collar and gives a negative reinforcement in the form of a uncomfortable feel in their nose. The problem is that dogs can develop, over time, a comfort level to the odor.

Effective Use Of A Chain Training Collar

Training collars or "choke collars," as they are more commonly known, are probably the most misunderstood training tool on the market. They can be abused by the owners and most dog owners do not know how to size it, fit it to a dog, or use it properly. Although we do not use chain training collars in our training program at Best Friend K-9 Training, we are going to spend a little time explaining it because people use it thinking it is a simple solution. It can do more harm to the dog, than it is worth.

As Buddy, the Police K-9, I think that I have the most experience with the effects of a choke collar. My background is simple. Think of the most hyperactive active kid you ever knew, the kid that would not take no for an answer. Yeah, I was equivalent to the kid that had ants in his pants and couldn't sit still for more than two seconds. I am the best example of a "HHHHADD" the Hyper-Hyper-Hyper-Hyper Active Deficit Disorder Dog. *(We are explaining the choker collar because it can be used improperly and that is what we want to prevent)*. A Martingale collar is recommended as the best control collar because it is a mistake free training tool.

When Bill picked me up from the handler who was retiring, he did not know what he was in for (again). I remember that day well. The four-year old hyperactive mutt he brought home had been cooped up for one month in another four by 10 foot kennel like Jasper was. When I arrived at Bill's house, I was just happy to feel grass under my paws; the feel of freedom was just overwhelming. Bill had Jasper, (now retired and living a good quiet dog's life inside the house) who always came on command. When I got into Bill's backyard, I didn't want to listen to anyone. I knew how to listen and knew what the consequences were if I didn't. I knew all the commands, but I felt freedom — and it was a good feeling. I ran and ran with reckless abandon. Well after 15 minutes of being outwitted by this out of control four-legged beast, Bill went inside and cooled down. (He was getting smarter as his career progressed. Remember — "common sense!")

It was March and the pool looked quite refreshing after acting like a maniac — so I jumped in. Yep, right into the middle of his 33 foot pool. There was one problem though. I didn't realize that there was a pool cover under the six inches of water. Right down I went. I felt like a Comanche in quicksand. I was beside myself. My legs were packed in the cover, (thank God I didn't puncture it) and I couldn't move. Lower and lower I went, until that guy I was running from came out and just stood there. Boy … was I glad to see my savior. He had other thoughts because he just stood there looking at me. I really think he was contemplating whether or not to let me drown and cut his losses early. But no, he did the humane thing and rescued me. Bill realized that I was his ticket to being in the K-9 Unit for a few more years. He had to lasso me with a long leash and drag me out of the water, pool cover and all. Unfortunately, I had to pay a price and with the leash and the choker collar I already had on, and received a correction like I never received before. Once Bill had me on leash with a choker collar, I was his, or better said, "in deep dog poop." He had complete control of me, because he knew what he was doing. I then realized that my last handler never had the knack quite like Bill. The choker and leash are incredible training tools only if they are sized properly and used correctly.

The metal choker collar or training collar is used for control and correction (we will discuss correction in the next section). This is a humane tool for working with your dog if used properly. The general consensus of many dog trainers is that it is one of the most effect training methods. Believe it or not, the choker collar can be put on two ways, the right way and the wrong way. To start though, we must brief you on some basics: 1). the dog will always be on your left side. (This is the industry standard.); 2). you will always hold the leash with your right hand; and 3). your left hand will be used for praise or positive reinforcement.

We don't recommend food rewards. We do recommend a mild "correction" as a training tool. If you look at the most professional group of dogs in the world, i.e., Police K-9's, it only makes sense to do what they do. The main problem is, **most people don't know what they are doing with a "choker" and shouldn't**

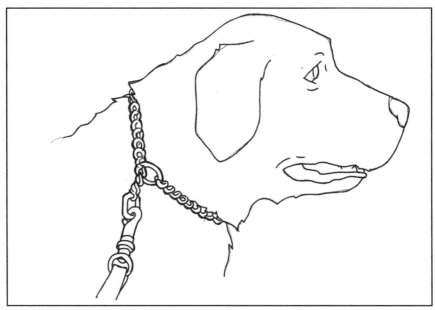

Proper Position Of Choker Chain

use it. Also look at any AKC competition whether it is obedience or a breed ring, all the dogs have choker collars on. I think the pros know what they are doing.

In many cases, folks that tell you how to train a dog, have no experience in dog training and couldn't teach a chimpanzee how to eat a banana. Dog trainers always hear from their clients that, "They say chokers are not good for dogs." My question to these people is, "Who is they?" They? — Who in the world is they? After asking them who "they" is, the person says, "Well you know." No we don't know who "they" is. If you rely on some unknown person who has no dog training experience, please get a grip on things and start looking at the real world of dogs. If you want to listen to "they," you and the dog will become very confused. *The reason for any confused dog is a confused owner. A confused dog is any dog that doesn't know how to behave in a home.*

Using the "chain choker" in a proper manner will never hurt your dog. That is why we are spending so much time explaining it. This is the most misunderstood training tool. Now that Bill has been using the Martingale collar, he finds that the Martingale is the most effective collar for the reasons stated earlier. If you as the owner are not comfortable with a piece of equipment and you do not completely understand how a piece of equipment is to be used, then learn about its proper use, or find an alternative.

What is the proper size of a choker collar? Measure the circumference of your dog's neck and add two or three inches. (See illustration previous page.) *Do not use a choker on a dog under six months old.* Use a Martingale collar instead. To measure a dog's neck size, use a piece of string and place it around the dog's neck. Make a mark indicating the circumference. Place that string against a ruler to get the neck size. The reason you add two to three inches to the neck size is because a choker that is the exact size of the neck will not fit over the dog's head. Again Martingale collars work best.

Proper placement of the metal choker collar: 1). Drop the chain through one of the rings. (We are explaining this because a lady once called Bill and said that the choke chain did not work. The @#&%$ lady said she couldn't get the one ring through the second ring so it would work properly. It's amazing how some dog owners can even take care of themselves much less having one of us around, — and they're even allowed to have kids. Go figure; 2). With your right hand facing you, place the chain over your fingers, with the ring on the end of the chain on the right side. The chain should look like a backward "P." (See illustration.) Now, with your dog on your left side place the collar over his face, and around his neck. (See illustration.) A common mistake is for the owner to turn and face the dog and the collar to go on backwards. (See illustration.) The dog should be on your left and just slide it over his head. The ring that attaches to the leash should loosen when you put slack on the leash; 3). The choker should be placed at the highest part of the dogs neck, just under the ears. Apply a little pressure to the leash to keep it snug and in place.

When you use the choker, make sure the dog is on your left side, (it's right shoulder next to your left leg). *To make a correction,* leave your leash slack and apply a sharp tug on the leash and say the word "NO" in a deep and affirmative voice. This will not hurt the dog but will reinforce the word "No" and lets the dog know that behavior is not acceptable. Your dog will feel some slight discomfort but will quickly forget it. You can be proportional with the tug with the size of the dog. For those "ding bats," that means a small tug for small dogs and a hard tug for larger dogs.

Again, we recommend the Martingale collar, but paid this much attention to the choker, because of its misuse.

With all this being said, and we only say it because the choker is a misunderstood and misused piece of equipment. *The Martingale collar is the way to go for several reasons:* 1). You can't put it on the wrong way; 2). You can tighten it up so it is snug around the dog's neck; 3). The sound of the chain is reinforcing, thus reminding the dog that trouble could be coming if it gets out .of line; 4) The Martingale collar will allow an effective correction regardless where the dog is, in relation to you, while the chain choker will only allow for an effective correction while the dog is on your left side; and 5). We make them and know that it's an extremely effective training tool.

Various Types Of Leashes

"My owners are Mike and Lee," said Cocco, and have been the best example of someone using the leash (or lead) in an effective manner. You see I'm a Chocolate Labrador and for the most part, that means serious trouble for whoever brings a cute puppy like me home. We don't stay as cute as we were as puppies and our actions, become simply idiotic to say the least if not controlled at an early stage of our life. There is no doubt that we are great dogs and great to have around, but please, understand who we are. We Labs, are a high-energy breed that like to horse around and need plenty of exercise. Don't forget we are hunting dogs and our job in life is to retrieve birds when they are shot out of the sky.

Well, one day when I was three months old, (I didn't think I was old enough to get into that much trouble) Lee told Mike, "He has to go," (he being me). So Mike looked up Best Friend K-9 Training for some serious assistance. Needless to say, the rest is history. I never knew a piece of fabric and a couple of snap rings could be so effective, along with the Martingale collar.

I'm going to tell you that I was never abused with the leash and especially NEVER HIT WITH A LEASH or with anything else. Mike and Lee learned that negative physical contact is never acceptable. What I learned was, the leash was a tool used in controlling me, and I needed some serious controlling. You will learn about correction in the next section, but let me say something, and I want you to remember it in the future, "correction" or reinforcement is a fact of life if you want a dog to become obedient. If your cute little puppy or grown dog has a lapse of memory, and runs from you and doesn't want to come to you, don't chase him with the leash in your hand. Some of you might remember back in the less politically correct days. There was a time when once in a while a youngster might need a belt across their butt. I heard that from Bill. If he saw his father with a belt in his hand, he knew that trouble was coming. The race began. Unfortunately for Bill, his father was faster than him but still the chase was on. Bill was always the loser. He was never abused but did need some swift punishment and he new he deserved it.

The same goes for us mutts. If you want us to come to you after you observed us commit an infraction, don't exhibit the leash (or to those of you who live in Reo Linda, as Rush Limbaugh would say, don't let us see the leash. We know what's coming if we see that leash, and are not going to hang around if we can help it. Also, if your dog runs from you and you call it back and it comes back on its terms, do not correct it. The dog did come back, but under its terms. You are sending a mixed message if you give it a correction.

The dog did what you wanted by coming and then you corrected it. This is not acceptable!! Think about the message you just sent. You must approach the dog and then correct it. It might take some time to chase it down, but never correct a dog after it comes to you. So chase it down if you are going to give it a correction.

Anyway, before I received my training, the leash meant nothing to me. It was used, just to pull me and I would just pull in the opposite direction. Remember, action-reaction.

The most effective and versatile training leash available is called THE ULTIMATE LEASH. This leash has eleven uses that make it extremely effective. Check it out at http://www.theultimateleash.com and look at the demonstration video. The Ultimate Leash can be used as a 1-foot, 2-foot, 3- or 6-foot leash. You can also secure your dog to a wire fence, post or a tree. You can make an emergency slip collar, or walk your dog hands free. Two dogs can also be walked on the same leash, and you can use it as a car restraint, or place it over your shoulder for off-leash use. One of the best things about the leash is that it is a 6-foot leash that can be adjusted to 3-feet, then adjusted again to 2- then 1-foot.

Let's say a few words about leashes. There are many varieties out there. There are short 8-inch, 12-, 18- or 36-inch leads, long 6-foot, 8- and 10-foot leads, and retractable leads. Again, look at the professional K-9 handler's use. The longest a leash should be is 6-feet, but only when the dog is completely under control. When heeling a dog you want only a 2-foot leash. When tracking with your dog you want a 20-25 foot leash. You will also want a 20-25 foot lead for teaching your dog distance commands. Most towns have ordinances that require a leash and that the leash has to be no more than 6-feet.

A good example of how a leash should be used is to use fishing as an example. As silly as it might sound, fishing can give you good lesson in dog training. When you catch a fish, where do you have most control of the fish? When you first catch a fish it is far away from you, swimming all over the place. Common sense will tell you that you have most control of a fish when you get it close to you so it can either be netted or pulled into the boat. The same works with a dog. Many people, who call for problem solving with their dogs, are usually victims of the wrong type of leash and their own ignorance. The longer the leash, the more out of control your dog will be. Some dogs, depending on how they are trained and by their basic nature, don't need a leash at all, or they can be on a loose leash and will stay next to you. The shorter the leash the more control you will have with your dog. Case closed.

When selecting a leash, remember that the longer the leash, the more trouble you will get yourself into with your dog. We don't need any encouragement in getting into trouble, and a long lead 6-foot or more will give us every opportunity to give you the most headaches imaginable.

Correction "Check"

Well, up to now, I (Buddy, the Police K-9) have been the best example of a mutt getting into trouble. I think that the reason Bill and I got along so well was because he was a lot like me when he was kid growing up. Correction was a fact of life for me and might have to be a fact of life for your dog at least during the early phases of training. (Let me emphasize that a correction is only a sharp tug, on the leash. It is simply reinforcement. In Police K-9, we call that a "check.") The "check" does not mean that you are dragging your dog by the neck or hanging it either. You see, the more consistent you are with the training at the start of your relationship with your hound, the fewer problems you will have in the future. That is something most people don't understand. Sure, it might feel uncomfortable to us, but as a result of the correction, the dog learned a lesson from it, and *you will be better off for being firm with your dog.* The dog simply learns what unacceptable behavior is, and you learn how to control your dog.

When you were a child, or in raising your own children, a price had be paid for doing something wrong. If there was no consequence for bad action, someone had to suffer and it was usually the mom and dad. Correction should be a learning experience for everyone involved. As most parents say, "It hurts me more than it hurts you," and that might be the case in giving a correction to your poor little Fido. But be consistent and never give up correcting bad behavior. Remember, correction should not be abusive, but a reminder of bad behavior. And remember that bad behavior is never acceptable. The word correction or "check" sounds harsh but it really isn't. For most dogs, a physical reinforcement is what we understand.

Correction should never be aggressive and not done in anger. That goes for both kids and dogs. Don't forget that the correction can only be used with a Martingale collar, chain collar or e-collar. A correction with a chain collar can only be effective it the dog is on your left side and the collar is set properly. A correction with a Martingale collar will be effective regardless of where the dog is.

Earlier, Jasper made reference to being as consistent as possible. Apply consistency here more than in any other area of training. DO NOT ABUSE CORRECTION!!!. If you do abuse your dog, you will suffer in the long run. At the same time, do not be timid about using correction. This is where common sense must prevail. *Do not act with your emotions.* Also, use a level of correction that fits the size of your dog. A larger dog will require a firmer tug than a smaller lap dog.

Correction or giving a check (sometimes called a jerk) is accomplished when the leash is attached to the choker or Martingale collar and a sharp tug is applied. Remember, with a choker on correctly, the dog must be on your left side to have any effect. Leave a little slack in the leash and apply a sharp jerk like a snapping type action. Remember that the force used, will be dependent on the size of the dog. (Please note: Bill has trained more dogs than he can remember, and has never injured a dog or heard of a dog being injured by using proper correction.) Some trainers will not use a choker on a few breeds, some will use a fabric choker (the Martingale), and that's OK based on individual preference. I can assure you that Bill has never had a problem with any dog group that he's trained. He does not use "chain" Martingale collars or chokers on dogs with neck issues so please ask your vet or kennel club which dogs should not be using a choker. (A Grey Hound, Italian Grey Hound, Whippet, are a couple of breeds that should not have a chain choker on.) A fabric "Martingale collar" is a must because these breeds have a head that is the same size of the neck and could easily slip from a standard collar. Just use common sense in every aspect of your training and especially with correction. Over and over, Bill has heard, "They say that you shouldn't use a choker on a dog!" OK, we have a couple of questions about that.

Don't forget our discussion earlier. That's right, the discussion where we asked who "they" are. Again: 1). Who are "They?" and; 2). What is their training experience? No doubt, anything can be abused. We are only reinforcing the proper use of the choke. This is why we recommend the "Martingale collar."

A common problem with dog owners is that they usually just tug on a dog. Remember your high school physics class, when the teacher taught you about the principle of "for every action, there is an equal and opposite reaction." I think that's how it goes. Well the same principle applies to dogs. If you just pull on a dog, the dog will usually pull in the opposite direction. Nothing gets accomplished except both of you will get upset with the situation. You end up having a tug of war with the dog and it's a good bet that the dog will win.

Correction or sharp tug (check) is not used by itself. Along with the check you will say "NO," in the sternest and deepest voice that you have. The dog must associate an action — CHECK — with a word — "NO." Eventually, the dog will associate the word NO when doing something wrong and will respond without the use of a check or correction. Ladies, this will be a challenge. Please do not scream at the top of your lungs at your dog. We dogs don't understand what's going on. (For all your dog knows, you sound like your pants are on fire and your calling for help.) Use correction with patience. You and your dog will be better off for it. Take a deep breath and lower your voice to the correction tone or I mean business tone.

Take it from me, Buddy the hyperactive Police K-9, be consistent with using correction. Yeah, I was a free spirit, but learned how to harness that energy into a positive action, and as a team, Bill and I had a great and successful career together, taking a bite out of crime, literally.

One final comment on choke collars. The next time you get a chance, go to an American Kennel Club dog show or watch one on TV, look at the collars the handlers use on the dogs. Every dog that is being shown in the ring has a "show collar" on which is placed very high on the neck of the dog. That show collar is a choker which is very thin. Granted the handler knows how to use it, and it is your responsibility to learn how to use a choker if that is the route you want to take for training. Speaking about Show Dogs, we have had many AKC Judges and Professional Handlers purchase our Martingale Collars for their dogs when they are not in the ring.

After all this is said, we recommend that you use a quality Martingale collar, where you cannot get into trouble.

Patience With Your Dog

Well, I'm **Kizzy,** one of the dogs that requires an extra dose of patience. It's not that I'm stupid, to the contrary — being a Mastiff is a great life. Sometimes, I'm just a little dopey. My masters, Henry, Maryanne, and Henry Jr., have shown the patience of a saint that has made the difference in the success of my training.

Well, this guy (Bill the trainer) showed up at my house to straighten me out. As I saw it, he just didn't understand my problem. Here I am a cute little puppy, three months old and pushing 65 pounds. You need a lot of energy to move that much weight at that age. I was never in the mood for training. They wanted me to sit and I would lie down. They wanted me to lie down and I would roll over. I wasn't being bad; it's just that I was lazy. Well with the attentiveness of Bill and the patience of my three masters, I was able to comprehend what this thing called training was all about. They never gave up on me. PATIENCE!! Yeah, it might have taken me a little longer than the usual mutt, (which might make me sound stupid), but I did learn, thanks to the patience of my three masters. They also made the training fun.

When it comes to training us canines, remember that you must be the winner in every obedience training situation. DO NOT GIVE UP ON TRAINING, because, whoever gives up first, loses. If a session requires that you do something 10 times in a row to get it right, then you have to do it 11 times, just for good measure. It just makes sense. When it comes to play time, we must win. When playing fetch, let your dog have the object in the end. The object is the reward for a good romp.

The next section talks about awareness and the effect it has on the training cycle. Awareness of a situation, and patience in dealing with it, should work hand-in-hand. If your trusted little friend is being plain old bad, then action is the only solution. You must have the patience to stay with a situation long enough until your dog learns what it is that you want from it. If for instance, you're trying to teach your dog to sit. If he doesn't do it the first time, are you going to give up? Absolutely not! You're not going to give up until you are satisfied with the performance of your dog. Look, we like training about as much as most kids like going to school or taking a bath, unless you make it fun, (positive reinforcement). If training is not done correctly, don't expect a lot of progress at the beginning. Patience is a virtue that you must have when working with your dog. As said before, if it takes 10 times to show your dog how to sit, then you must do it 11 times. If you stop before the dog learns, then in effect it is doing a better job of training you then you are training the dog.

Another point to remember is that training must be a fun time for both of you. Make the training event an exciting part of your dog's day. Talk it up with your dog before training. Get your voice high and say, "Let's go train," you know, how a coach motivates a team. Build up the excitement.

Patience is not only used in the actual training environment. In a problem situation, patience must be exhibited by just taking a step back and looking at a situation, take a deep breath and then react. There should be no surprises on what we are capable of doing. Don't jump to conclusions when confronted with what appears to be a bad situation. Sure, bad behavior requires immediate action, but, if you are not sure about an incident or what action to take, don't react without thinking, because that reaction will usually be an overreaction. Be patient and think through a situation. We can't emphasize that enough. Dog's don't have the ability to apply patience to a situation. So it's up to you.

If the training session is not going as you planned, it is your fault. You're controlling the process and it is your responsibility to get the most out of it.

Awareness

"De-nial is not a river in Africa"

Hi, I am a Rottweiler named **Kalib,** or better known as a "block head." My owners had to have complete awareness of my ability to act in a very weird way. By that I mean I was not consistent with my actions. I had my moments of greatness, and my moments of great disappointment with AJ and Angie. This reminds me of a story I heard from Jasper, when he and Bill were working undercover one day, as a blind man and Seeing Eye dog. One day they were playing the role of a pan handler with a sign asking people for money to feed the dog. (Of course the sign had to be upside down). They were sitting on a staircase leading down to a subway waiting for a robbery suspect to arrive. Well, Officer Bill did not give himself the usual check down before they went out for the shift. He was in such a hurry to get to the location and lock up this bad dude, he forgot (lack of awareness) to remove his wristwatch. What blind man goes around with a crystal faced wristwatch on. To make matters worse, while he and Jasper were sitting there with the panhandling sign, he looked at the time on his watch while one lady put some money in the cup. The lady was even more unaware of the situation than Officer Bill was, because she saw him look at his watch and didn't even question it while she put the money in. (Don't worry, the money always went to a charity.)

Things can happen in the same manner with dog owners. You might see a situation but not fully comprehend it or even worse, not want to comprehend it or accept it. You're in denial. Sometimes you might even say, "That didn't just happen, did it?" It is your job as a dog owner to be continently aware of every situation you see with your dog. In other words don't be an "Air-Head."

Be aware of what both you and your dog are doing whenever you are together. When we talk around the pack, we find that most dog owners are not aware enough to give the proper amount of praise. Sure, correction is pretty swift, but how about a nice pat on the head for a job well done or just a nice pat on the head just for being buddies. *Where is it folks?* One thing that AJ and Angie do in a consistent way is that they are aware of every situation I get myself into. That is for both good and bad situations. I receive more than enough praise when I'm a good little (105 lbs. at nine months) puppy, and I receive my share of correction when I have a lapse of memory and am not so good.

You should be most aware of every situation during at the earliest stages of training. (Learn to read your dog and how it is reacting in its surroundings.) That is, the more effective you are at the beginning stages of training, the more consistency you develop in the process. This awareness will enhance the effectiveness of training for you and your dog. It is just a matter of conditioning the two of you together. Learn to develop habits together. We as dogs cannot reason situations, but we can become ingrained with what we are supposed to do. Don't forget that we can also untrain ourselves if you don't keep up with training.

A few years ago, there was a cute cartoon in the Sunday paper. Marmaduke is a very big dog, and was lying on the couch. The little kid that owned Marmaduke was talking to his friend and said, "I trained him, but he untrained himself." Many people see their once trained dog, starting to act up, or out of control. Well, those people must ask themselves a simple question. How did this happen? It happened because you were not aware of things going downhill real fast. If you blame the dog, like many people do, you obviously don't know much about dogs. Remember that you must be the leader of the pack. Training should be conducted every day even after the formal training stops. Once the training stops, the dog will regress. You are forewarned about what to expect with the future of your dog.

CHAPTER 5

Dog Training 101

Teaching Fido to do commands is quite simple. OK guys this is **Shasha** — yeah the dog from H@%$#!! Once my owner decided that training would be easier if they took the advice of a trainer, life for both of us became much easier. The problem is that you humans don't know what the word "simple" means when it comes to us dogs. You try to apply reason with us and that simply doesn't work, or, you give up and complain how stupid we are. You see we don't think or reason like humans and believe it or not, we never will. Training should be simple, easy and a pleasure for everyone involved.

DON'T ATTEMPT TO NEGIOATE WITH THE PET DOG. WHEN YOU TRY TO NEGOIATE, YOU WILL LOSE IN THE PROCESS. TAKING THE POLITICALY CORRECT APPROACH WILL BE A LOSING BATTEL EVERY TIME.

When training your dog stay focused and be as consistent as possible. "Don't ever give up!!!" Training involves endurance with some dogs. Some dogs are fast learners, and some dogs are not. Just as there are some less intelligent people, that, when you tell them something, you might as well be talking to a fire hydrant. So is the same for dogs. You can tell fairly quickly what the ability level of your pet is by taking into some considerations.

Some things to consider before you train your dog are, Breed category, does the dog have a job that they were bred for? How old is the dog? How smart are you and can you handle the job? This is not to sound sarcastic, but again, I'm here to explain the plain truth, and not be politically correct. We won't give you the soft answers or sugar coat anything I am going to say. Plain and simple, *"Some people should not be dog owners!!!"*

There are three types of people in the world. Which category do you fall into? We give these examples because it should help you understand how you can improve your relationship with your dog:

1). *"Those people that make things happen."* These are really good dog owners that can get their dog to do anything. They are taking the time and energy to work with their dog;

2). *"Those people that watch things happen."* These are people that might be good dog owners, but don't have a handle on how to train it. They realize that they are not doing enough to train the dog and blame themselves and realize that their furry friend can't learn by itself, and then there are;

3). *"Those people that wonder what just happened."* These poor souls are dog owners that do not have a clue and do the blame game that everything is the dog's fault. In reality, they are at fault and can't see it. "Clueless" would be the best description for these people.

If you say that your dog is un-trainable, the next time you're in the bathroom, look in a mirror and focus on the real culprit. *ALL DOGS CAN BE TRAINED, NOT ALL HUMANS CAN BE TRAINED though!! Case Closed!!* Yep folks plain and simple, we have met more ignorant people out there that blame all problems on the dog. Sorry to say this but if you have a problem with your dog, the problems in all likelihood start with YOU!! Again, if you get 10 dog trainers in a room together and ask them the same question, you will probably get 10 different answers, except for one specific question. That question is, *"What is the worst part about dog training?"* The answer from all 10 trainers will be, *"The Owners!!!"*

Consider These Factors
Before You Start To Train Your Dog

The Breed. What breed category is your dog in? Example for the simple minded. If you have a sporting dog ie., Labrador Retriever, German Short Haired Pointer, Springer Spaniel, etc. be prepared to go through a battle unless you tire your dog out before training, or you are experienced with the breed. Then keep your dog tired during the day so they won't get into trouble in the house. All these dogs want to do is act like they have ants in their pants and move and pull and jump and move and pull and jump. That's what they are supposed to do. They are really great animals with a specific job to do. Get the picture? If they're in a house with nothing to do and nothing to play with, well, what do you expect? They are going to get into trouble. Whose fault is it? Certainly not the furry guy!! We don't know any better. Study the breed before training. It will save a lot of aggravation in the long run.

Time Investment. You might ask at this point, what do you mean time investment, the last dog I had could do anything the first time I showed him. No two dogs are alike. K-9 Jasper and K-9 Buddy were as different as you could get. They could do the same things, but each had to be trained in different ways. (Jasper could be trained to perform a task the first time he was shown that task. Buddy on the other hand took 4, 5, 6, 7, 8, 9, sometimes 10 to do it before he even began to realize what he was supposed to do.)

The goal is to realize that and capitalize on the strengths and weaknesses of every dog you own. If you're not prepared to spend at least 15 minutes a day working with your dog, then don't get involved in dog ownership much less training your dog. You will lose in the process and the dog will out smart you because you're not smart enough to see the value of working with your dog on a consistent daily basis. When it comes to the 15 minutes a day, try to do it in three, five-minute increments. For those of you from Bayonne that means five minutes in the morning, five minutes in the afternoon and five minutes in the evening.

Training Your Dog Is A Life Long Commitment

To many people, training a dog sounds simple. That is a correct statement if you know what you are doing. As a dog trainer with 30 years of experience, Bill can train any dog in full Basic and part of Advanced Obedience in a, two-hour session. This would include a 15 minute Sit, Down, Stay, Come, Heel, Hand commands, teaching the word No, and distance control. Believe me when I say this, it is not a mark of him being a genius. He clearly isn't. The fact is that he has so much experience at doing it. The one thing he has never been able to do is to train the owner in a two-hour session.

Even to train an owner what to do in two hours, when Bill has given them a fully trained dog is impossible, unless the owner has some level of experience. This is why we do not take dogs and train them and give them back to the owner. It is simply harder to train the owner.

Training your dog doesn't stop after the dog receives its initial training. Working your dog is a constant work in progress and when you understand that, the both of you will be better off. Granted, after a while, it will take less time to reinforce the process with Fido, but it does take a commitment and consistency. After basic obedience or any formal training, plan on spending 10-minute sessions with your dog three or four times a week. The best is to incorporate training into your daily routine. Sit your dog before it goes out or comes into the house. Make your dog lay down in a specific area once or twice a day. Remember, positive reinforcement is an extremely important part of the process.

Training should be fun. If you are not planning on having fun during the training, how do you expect your dog to have a good experience with it either? Get your dog excited with your voice tone. When you see the progress, it will become more and more fun for the both of you. Your excitement level will trickle down the lead.

Don't give up!!! No matter how difficult it seems, do not give up when training your dog. He who gives up first loses. It kind of works the same way with kids, doesn't it? Ever see a kid in the store that wants candy and starts crying. The parent has no intention of giving in, but after five minutes of hearing the two legged critter scream, the kid gets his way and has won the battle. (What happens the next time the kid goes into the store? The same thing happens all over again.) You must always win the battle with your pet when it comes to training the first time. Keep doing it until both of you get it right. (During play time the dog always wins though. We will discuss that later.)

The first command that we want to do is **Sit.** Sit is the easiest command to teach a dog because believe it or not they already know how to do it. Now you want to teach the dog to do it when you want them to.

An important part of dog training involves your communication with the dog. *Remember a "High Tone" voice will be used for praising the good that your dog is doing. A "Medium Tone" voice will be used for the commands and a "Deep Tone" voice for correction when the dog is disobedient. Remember: Correction is not for a dog that makes a mistake or might be confused.*

DO NOT use the Dog's name when giving commands except for the "Come" command.

SIT

1). Hold the leash in your right hand.

2). The dog must be on your left side

3). Say "SIT" in a mid range tone and put your left hand on his hind rump and push down, and at the same time pull up with the leash with your right hand. The dog will sit. Now give the dog a pat on its head and give praise with a higher pitched voice, "Good boy or girl."

Keep it there for 15 minutes. If your dog moves keep doing it until you win. The dog will learn if you don't give up. It might be a battle of wills. Whoever gives up first, loses.

The sit command will show you and your dog that you have control of the situation. If you do this correctly, your dog will understand that you are the leader. Remember, don't give up.

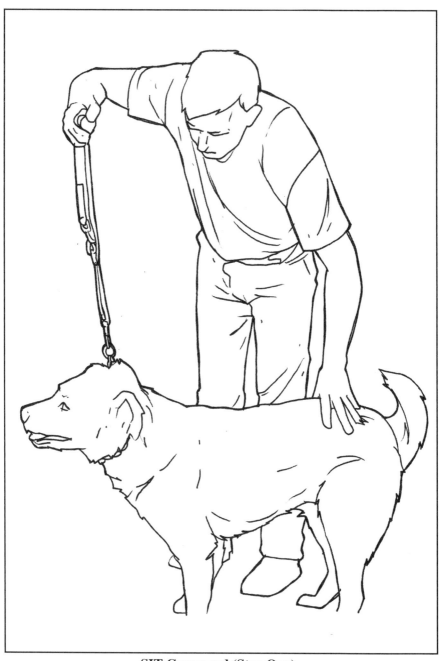

SIT Command (Step One)

SIT Command (Step Two)

DOWN

1). Keep the leash in your right hand. The dog must be on your left side and in a sit position.

2). Hold the leash with your right hand close to the dog right next to the collar.

3). Pull the leash down to the ground, and at the same time say "Down" in a mid range tone.

4). If this is difficult, place your left hand over the front shoulder, (over the solid bone part, not the back or neck) and push down. If all else fails, gentle pull the front legs forward and say, "Down." Give the dog a pat on the head and positive praise.

5). Hold your hand over the shoulder and put enough pressure on it to keep the dog down.

Down is one of the hardest commands to teach a dog. If you give up and feel it's too hard, you have lost a major issue and the dog will remember that.

A good point to remember about the "Down" command is that the down position is a position of submission. That means that many dogs will not go into a "down" because they are being forced into a position that they feel is submissive. They feel as though they have lost on this issue. (Some dogs will do it very easily.) Again, it's somewhat like watching a nature show on TV where there are pack animals. If you have ever observed a fight for leadership of the pack, the winner of the fight pins the loser to the ground, usually with the neck. The winner becomes the "Alpha Leader." To the same extent, you are winning this issue with your pet and becoming the "Alpha Leader." This lets the dog know you are the boss. If all else fails, (and this is the only time I will tell you to do this), hold a treat in your right hand and draw the dog into the down. Do not give the dog the treat until it complies with the command and stays there for a couple minutes. The only time we use a treat is to coax the dog down. When the dog learns this, make the size of the treat smaller and smaller until you have none and then use positive reinforcement.

The earlier in the dog's life that you teach it to "Down," the easier it will be able to teach the command.

DOWN Command (Step One)

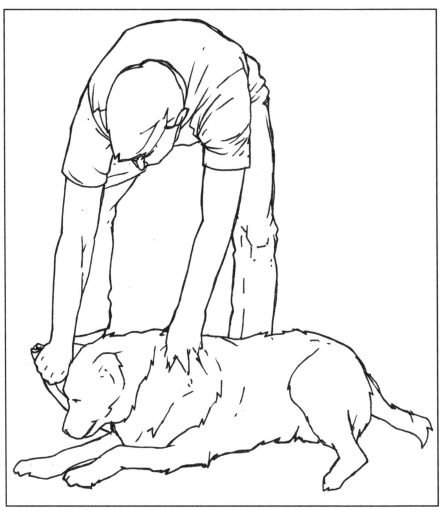

DOWN Command (Step Two)

STAY COMMAND

How do some people make it look so easy to get their dog to Sit-Stay or Down-Stay. Well it's like anything else. It takes a lot of practice.

This is **Olive** talking and if you asked Bill, he would say that I am probably as dumb as a box of rocks. I'm a Peak-a-poo (Pekinese-Poodle mix) and I do have to admit, I was a little dense, but mom, Bills wife Debbie just loved me.

"SIT-STAY" Command (Step One)

I'm her protector and whenever Bill comes to give her a kiss, I'm on his leg like in the Breakstone Yogurt commercial. I guess if I were Bill, I wouldn't be a fan of mine either.

"SIT-STAY" Command (Step Two)

To resolve this problem, mom taught me how to "Sit." Then she would make me sit while on leash, holding the leash with her left hand and saying, "stay," holding her right hand out in front of the dog. She would then take one step in front of me, stepping out with her right foot. As she did this she would turn towards me and hold out her right hand in front of my face. She would practice this for a few days until I got it right and then she took two steps in front of me and continued with this ritual until she was about 10 feet from me. It took a while but it worked. Soon Bill was able to kiss his wife and not have to worry about getting a bite on the leg.

Practice makes perfect, especially when training a dog in the "Stay" command. Many times the dog wants to follow you when you take that step forward. Remember when we discussed about not giving up even if it took 10 times to do something. If you keep doing something with your dog long enough, your dog will learn. If I can learn something like "Stay" then any dog can do the same.

COME COMMAND

Come is probably the most important command you will teach your dog and for good reason. I am **Zack** and as a Police K-9 I loved to be off leash. Freedom was a very fulfilling experience whenever I had the chance. I do admit that I was a pretty decent Police K-9 and do know the "Come" command. It took a while to learn it though.

My handler was Eric, who was a great guy. It was me who was a little stubborn about coming to him when called. In Police K-9 we would do an exercise called a "Recall." This was when a dog was sent after a "Bad Guy," and if the "Bad Guy" surrendered by stopping, the handler would call the dog back to him. The two would approach the "Bad Guy," the K-9 was told to sit, and the apprehension was made without a bite being taken out of the perpetrator. That wasn't fair to me since I thought that biting a bad guy was my job. Yes, biting bad guys was my job, but under very controlled situations and when a bad guy resisted arrest. But I had to learn this lesson the hard way.

When we started out with this exercise one day after graduating from the academy, the scenario would go like this. The perpetrator runs away firing blanks "Bang! Bang! Bang!" The handler would give the command "Go, Get Him" and the chase was on. Being that the fastest a man can run in a sprint is about 18 mph, it doesn't take long for the dog to catch up, sprinting at about 32 mph, so, the handler has to think fast and the dog has to react to commands in a split second. If the perpetrator surrendered, Eric would yell, "Zack, No, Come, Heel" (Notice that my name was used in the come command.)

Bill was the acting perpetrator on this particular day and I wasn't up for taking commands and I decided that he wouldn't mind taking a "Hit" (bite) or two or three or four or five or six or seven, on the arm. (Of course his arm was wrapped in protective layers of leather and burlap.) I didn't think coming back to Eric was all that important at the time and decided that I would take a few liberties. This happened about six times when there should have only been one bite. Bill was pretty well fed up and decided that this dog isn't going to bite him again. A long rope was retrieved and attached to my collar. (The nylon rope was probably about 75 feet and if stretched would extend to about 78 feet.) Eric tied the other end to a bumper of a truck.

The next exercise went like this. Bill ran out to about 80 feet and Eric sent me to make the apprehension. You guessed it, I didn't stop and got the surprise of my life at 75 feet. Jumpin' Jehosaphat, what in the world just happened to me? Before I knew it I was upside down and flipping around like a rag at the end of a stick. My neck felt like it stretched 10 inches and it seemed like my eyes just about popped out of their sockets. I obviously learned an important lesson the hard way.

Sometimes, learning isn't always a good experience even for Police K-9s. I was humbled and felt bad that I was made a fool of in front of my other K-9 buddies. After that experience, I made sure I listened to the command "Come" whenever Eric gave it. (But don't worry about my neck because it is one of the strongest muscles in my body.)

This is not how you will train your dog to come, but I thought you would enjoy the story. You will eventually work up to using a long rope 25-50 feet to keep you and the dog together.

To start the "Come" command, put the dog in a "Sit" on your left side and give the "Stay" Command. (You can also start from a "Down-Stay" but "Sit-Stay" is easier in the beginning." You will step out with your right foot, holding your open right hand in front of the dogs face. You will then, (while facing the dog) step back one pace and stand there. Your hand will be out on your right side so the dog can see it. In training your dog, this is the only time you want to use its name. Your command for the dog to come will be: "Fido, Come, Come, Come" (High pitched excited voice) and pulling the lead towards you. Then say with an excited praise tone say, "Good Boy" (or Girl), "What a Good Boy," as the dog comes and at the same time giving the dog allot of excited petting and rubbing. If the dog does not instinctively come to you, you can take a step or two back, or kneel down on one knee, which usually will draw the dog into you. Some trainers sit the dog in front of the handler, facing each other while some sit the dog on the left side with both facing forwards. Do what is recommended by your trainer.

When you master this short exercise, you would extend the stay distance to 10 feet, master that and incrementally go to 25 feet in 5-foot measurements. Another exercise is to use a 25-foot lead and walk the dog in an open area. Let the dog walk around at the longest distance of the line and then call it to you. When the dog comes to you, you must make it seem like a big deal by getting excited and petting and rubbing the dog all over, then give positive praise reinforcement with a high pitched, "Good Dog, Good Dog." If the dog doesn't come initially, just give a little tug on the lead and if necessary pull it to you and when it gets to you, give a lot of praise and positive reinforcement.

HEEL COMMAND

There is nothing more impressive than to watch someone walking their dog on the left side of the handler and the dog is just there mimicking each step the owner takes. That is called having total control of your dog.

This is **Kalib** speaking. I'm the Rottweiler who at nine months weighed 90 pounds and thought I should walk my owners instead of them walking me. The heel command can be a more difficult command to teach a dog, but there are some tips that you can apply that will make the process easier.

When AJ and Angie, (my owners), would walk me they used a six-foot leash. In my mind that meant that I could walk out in front of them because I was never taught to do it differently. We're not mind readers and will do whatever we want because we don't know better. A long leash means less control by the dog owner.

To start the process of training a dog to heel, you must have the right equipment. Sure you can learn with a "head halter" or a "pinch collar," but what happens when you take those things off the dog. The dog goes back to it's usual unruly behavior. Cut your losses early and use a "Martingale collar." The Martingale collar and a short leash that is two feet is what you want to use. The Martingale collar will make the dog uncomfortable if it pulls. The two-foot leash will keep it close to you.

1). To start, place the Martingale collar around the dog's neck and keep it snug (2-3 fingers) and positioned high on the dog's neck. Position the dog on your left side. The proper heel position would have the dog walking on the left side of the handler. The dog's right shoulder will be next to the handlers left leg.

2). Hold the leash in your right hand. This allows your left hand to be used to positively reinforce the dog with a little petting on the top of the head. Remember, you do not want to give too much positive reinforcement because that will distract the dog and cause it to break from the heel command.

3). Start the dog from the "sit" position. By having the dog sit, it is establishing in its mind that you are doing obedience.

4). After the dog sits, you will do three things at the same time. That's right the same time. You might want to practice this a couple times before doing it with your dog: 1). You will say "Heel;" 2). You will tap the side of your left leg with your left hand; and 3). You will step out with your left leg. The reason you step out with your left leg is because you want your dog to follow your leg. (When you give the "Stay" command, you step out with your right leg, which, after your dog learns this, will not move when the right leg moves out first.)

5). Step forward and take three or four steps and then put your dog in a sharp sit. If the dog doesn't stop and sit, you will pull up sharply on the leash and say "Sit." Do this several times, and then take a break.

6). If the dog is having a hard time doing this, start the dog in a heel and take five steps and make a sharp left turn. If the dog is slightly ahead, just turn left and don't worry about the dog. They will eventually get it. If you step on the foot, don't worry about it, the dog will get the point and back up. Also a sharp left knee to the chest while making the left turn will also work.

Remember that this is not something that is learned during the first lesson or practice session. Keep doing it until you get it right. Practice — Practice — Practice.

Before you do obedience, do a dry run without the dog a couple of times, so you can get it right without any distractions.

Bringing A New Baby Into A House That Already Has A Dog

Hey, kids are great and it's one of life's joys to bring a new baby into a household. When there is a dog involved, the new parents can take a few precautions that will hopefully help in the transition of the little one being introduced. This is **Casey** and I'm waiting for my new brother to come into this world. My mom and dad have had me for three years. I've always been a good dog, just as they have been good masters to me. They had a trainer come over when I was young and everything has worked out great.

After learning about the new baby, they asked the trainer to come over to help them introduce the little one to me. That was a very smart thing to do.

About a month before the baby was due, I watched mom and dad carrying a small doll wrapped in a blanket around the house. When doing this they would ignore me. At first I felt a little funny about that but after they put the doll down, I would get petted. They would do this periodically during the day. They would walk, sit on the sofa and sit at the dining room table. I was allowed to walk around them but was told to lay down most of the time. I learned that I couldn't nose around them when they had the doll.

After taking mom to the hospital for the arrival of our new baby, dad brought home a small baby blanket. It smelt kind of different. It was an odor that I never smelt before. I walked to dad and smelt around a little bit. The smell appeared to be somewhat soft. He let me in the area and then told me to lie down in my special place. He brought home a new blanket each day until my new baby brother came home.

When mom and dad would hold the baby, I was allowed to walk around them, but I was never allowed to smell it. I could smell it well enough from where I was. I was allowed to lie down near them. That way I didn't feel jealous.

It wasn't for a few months that the baby was allowed to pet me. I guess it could have been sooner but that is how the trainer told them to do it.

Over time, my new brother and I became great friends and our life together has been the best. Take time to follow these examples with your new baby. Don't expect that introducing a new baby to a dog without proper training will be easy. It could happen that everything will go well, but why take a chance.

CHAPTER 6

Problem Solving Issues

Jumping

J umping on a person is a problem that many dogs go through, and for several reasons. This is **Bear** talking. I had this problem at an early age. As a young pup, I was always an excitable little guy and whenever my masters (Bill and Debbie) came around me, I would be petted and the excitement in me grew to a level that I would want to jump up to them so I could be closer to them. I never wanted to be away from them. I would follow them to the door when they left the house and I could hear the car leaving. When they returned home I could hear the car coming down the street and I was waiting at the door when they came in the house. My greeting to them was to jump up on them. In my excitement, I just wanted to see them.

They took several steps to solve this problem right after they noticed that a problem was developing. They were very *"aware"* of the situation. The primary reason for my jumping was that I wanted the constant affection from them. I loved it as most of your pets do.

Step #1. Lessen the constant affection that you give your dog during certain situations, such as leaving the house or coming into the house. When I noticed that the petting and rubbing had stopped during certain situations, I did not look forward to it as much as when I used to. My level of excitement dropped dramatically. Don't worry folks, I still knew they loved me.

(Note) I remember very well when mom and dad came home one night and I jumped up to greet them. Mom didn't want to tolerate my jumping so a swift knee to my chest solved the problem very quickly. You will not hurt a medium to large dog with a knee to their chest.

Step#2. When mom and dad were leaving the house they ignored me. I know this might sound like they are bad masters, but in reality they made sure that I had to earn their affection. Eventually I didn't bother them when they left the house. As they were getting ready to leave they also gave me the down command, so I wouldn't bother them as they were getting ready.

Step #3. When they returned home, they ignored me again as they walked into the house. After a while I learned that I needed to earn their affection in certain situations, before they petted me. Now, as a result of this behavior on their part, I don't even get up when they return home. Now as they walk into the house, they call me, I get up to see them.

Step #4. When having company over, it is totally unacceptable for any dog to jump up on company when they enter your home or any time that the company is in your home. That's right. You heard it right from a dog. People who are invited into your home deserve the courtesy of a peaceful visit to your home. Invited guests are your priority. Your dog is expected to have manners.

If your dog is completely unmanageable when people come into your home, then put the mutt in another room or a crate. (By the way, that behavior is your fault.) It is as simple as that. Another solution that worked on me was to train your dog to sit in a certain area until the company enters your home. You then ask the invitees if they want to meet the dog and you can let the dog greet them. Remember, do not let your dog jump up on someone invited into your home. Practice this with friends before having your guests over.

Teaching a dog to sit is a simple command that can be used when people are around. If it obeys then you can let it up to greet everyone. If it acts like a maniac then put it in a sit again or remove it to another room and close the door.

House Breaking And Urinating In The House

Urinating in the home is one of the most offensive things a dog can to its owner. The problem of a dog urinating in the house usually develops with the owner. The owner just didn't take enough time to take care of the situation at the beginning of the relationship with their dog. Remember when I told you about when Bill brought me home and the first thing he did was to walk me to the area in the yard that was to be my bathroom. Well that really sunk in. After we returned to the house he walked me right outside again. This second walk was for good reason. We dogs like to be lazy and just in case I didn't complete my business when I was supposed to, he made sure I did it the second time.

After returning to the house, he let me explore a little bit, then I had to go into my cage in the kitchen. (The kitchen was my room for one year. They put gates up in the entrance ways.) Remember when I arrived at my new home, it was about 11pm and everyone was tired including me. The time of day didn't stop the initial training.

For the next few days mom and dad walked me every two hours with the same routine. If I had an accident, they cleaned it with a paper towel, and brought the paper towel to my outside bathroom. I could smell where I was supposed to go. The soiled area was then cleaned with an odor neutralizing solution. The day after I moved in, Bill bought an one-foot picket fence from "Lowes" (Home Depot doesn't carry them) with some stakes and placed it around my bathroom area. You see, some dogs aren't that bright and will wonder to relieve themselves, because we can't differentiate boundaries. All grass looks the same as does leaves on the ground. So by marking the area, I could see where I was expected to go. Now it's a routine and I could walk there blindfolded.

Older dogs that have not been house broken create quite a challenge. Trainers have told me that smaller dogs have this problem more than larger dogs. This is partly because owners of smaller dogs seem to coddle the little creatures. In more specific terms they are just plain old spoiled.

The best course of action for training an older dog to go outside is; **#1** Clean all areas that the dogs has relieved itself with an odor neutralizing solution. Make sure you do a really good job on wood floors as well as carpet. They are hardest to clean. (DO NOT USE AMONIA) This will be a big task and might require getting rid of carpeting. The odor of urine attracts us back to that area. **#2** Try to do this next part on a weekend. Walk your pet every hour in the area you want it to relieve itself. From a prior accident clean-up, put the paper towel in the dogs bathroom area prior to walking the dog. This will attract its attention. Now this is the hard part. Stay there until it relieves itself. If after a half hour and you're twiddling your fingers, and that bleeping #@%&$*&!'' dog isn't doing anything, then return to the house and walk in, then walk right out to the designated area, until it goes. Hey, you created this problem over a period of time, so get used to the idea that the problem isn't going to solve itself over night. Keep doing this until the dog gets the idea. If need be, crate the dog for unattended periods in the house. And keep it in the kitchen until it is house trained.

Chewing

Ah .... this is an interesting subject for me. This is **Jasper** talking and I have a little story to tell. I was never a problem in the house. I started out house trained and never chewed anything but my chew bone, food, or the reward towel I would get when I found a drug stash just like I was supposed to. And then again, on one of the more interesting days, I would bite a perpetrators body part when the bad guy would attempt to resist arrest. Go figure, that happened about 35 times during my career. One day Bill was getting ready to go out. He put on a very expensive "Mercedes Benz" shirt that was given to him by his mother. Bill was looking in the mirror to spruce up and comb his hair, (when he had hair) and saw a tan spot on the shirt. He looked down at the spot and saw that a hole was chewed in the material. Well you know how timing is everything, I just happened to be sitting outside the bathroom door when he looked at me, and I couldn't hide my reaction. I put my head down in a guilty manner and started to do a military low crawl thinking I might get away. Bill was too smart for me. He knew

I must have done this act of stupidity shortly before and yep, I knew a correction was-a-comin'. Needless to say, I never chewed anything again except for my chow and a chew toy.

I don't know what made me do it. I guess it just seemed like the right thing to do at the time. Stupid me, because I should have known of the consequences that were coming. Maybe I should have jumped up and acted like nothing happened when he looked at me, but we dogs can't reason to the point of trying to cover something up. Unlike politicians, dogs will always tell the truth.

If your dog has a persistent chewing issue, we have a few things you can do. These are in no specific order.

- Remove all tempting items from the area the dog is in. Remember most times it just takes a little "common sense."

- Put the little bugger in a crate. Hey this stuff isn't rocket science. Don't forget that you don't have to be told how to do something by a dog trainer. You're the one who is supposed to have common sense. You can do a little problem solving yourself.

- Place plenty of play toys in the dog's area. Don't forget to rotate toys since playing with the same stuff day in and day out can be a little boring.

- Dogs are always going to get into some trouble. Most of the time, if you are one step ahead of us, you can alleviate many bad situations.

- Give the dog a correction for its misbehavior! I received a swift and very quick check (described earlier). I understood what I did wrong and I made sure it wasn't going to happen again.

A teething puppy can be annoying especially since their teeth seems like they could be from a Piranha's mouth. They are very sharp and very small and the puppy is not sure what to do with them. Play biting is not acceptable. For puppies that are teething, try this. Take an old washcloth and wet it. Roll it up and place it in the freezer. Give it to the dog. It will sooth their gums and give it something to dig it's teeth into instead of your skin.

Pulling

When it comes to dogs that "Pull" they are only telling you "I want to be the leader. I'm **Raspy** (who knows where that name came from) and I'm a Husky and it's good to meet you. Pulling, or wanting to be the leader of the pack, is a trait of any dog, but for me and similar breeds, we have perfected it. It's our job. When a person brings one of us into their home they have to realize that we were bred to pull sleds on snow. Again, why wouldn't someone research the breed before getting a dog?

Solutions for pulling cannot be explained easily, but we will attempt to help you out.

When Bill and I first met, I thought that this guy would be easy. You see, my owner had a harness on me. Go figure those idiots. What would they expect? Harnesses only make it easy to pull. The material over our shoulders distributes the pressure of the leash which is attached to the top of the harness on my back, making it very comfortable to pull. They also had a 6-foot leash.

The first thing Bill did was to put a Martingale collar on my neck. He snugged it up at the top of my neck. He then put on The Ultimate Leash and adjusted it to two-feet long. At first I instinctively tried to resist by pulling, but quickly realized that life on a short leash and a tight collar was very uncomfortable. If I attempted to pull, Bill showed my owner that they should apply a quick and swift check or jerk on the leash. The harder I tried to pull the stronger the consequence.

Some suggestions to stop a pulling dog:

- Go back to basics. You read the section on how to heel your dog. Now practice it. Whenever your dog starts to regress just go back to the basics and start all over again. If your dog already learned how to heel, it shouldn't take long to get them up to speed again. It's up to you.
- Use a short leash which should be two-feet and the dog's front right leg should be next to your left leg.
- Use a Martingale collar. Remember that these collars must be snug and placed at the top of the neck.

- If the dog consistently pulls try walking five steps then make a left turn. Walk into the dog and don't worry if you step on their paws. You can also walk five steps and stop with a quick check to the dog and make it sit. Continue this until it works. Practice makes perfect. Do it every day for 10 minutes and you will see results. If you don't see any results after a week then you are doing something wrong.

Pulling is a situation where there are many solutions. A book could be written on the subject alone. Many times it takes an experienced trainer to resolve a situation that you allowed to happen.

Aggression

Aggression in dogs is a situation that there will be NO GUARANTEED SOLUTION. This is **Bear** talking again. I remember when Bill came home from a training session where the lady called and explained that her 120-pound Rottweiler was showing signs of aggression. Her main concern was that she had a nine-year- old son in the house. Bill was pretty ticked off because some people put their aggressive dogs ahead of their own family when it comes to their feelings.

The training apparently didn't go very well because Bill had worked up a sweat. That has never happened before. When he arrived at the lady's house, he laid his eyes on the biggest Rottweiler he ever saw. The dogs name was "Vicious," and it was no wonder why. The head of Vicious was the size of a steering wheel.

Being a cautious trainer, Bill told the lady to put his training collar on the dog along with his leash. He wanted to make sure the equipment wouldn't fail. Bill wasn't stupid so he had her do the dirty work. The lady did that and Bill took Vicious outside. For a few seconds the dog seemed OK. Bill was petting its monstrous head making sure he didn't take his eyes off the dog with that big steering wheel staring back. The dog refused to look away. Eye contact is very important in the animal world. The one who looks away first is determined to be the "second fiddle" or loser. It was a good thing he didn't take his eyes off the dog because after about 10 seconds all he could see was the back of the dogs throat with four canines coming at him at what seemed like the speed of Mario Andretti driving an Indy Race Car. That dog wanted a piece of Bill's head. That's what you call an aggressive dog.

Fortunately Bill had a tremendous amount of experience with aggressive dogs and lifted the dog off the ground with the leash. This is a worst case scenario. Fortunately Bill weighed 210 pounds but even he could barely handle the situation. He was able to drag the dog onto its back and he grabbed its neck holding it to the ground with a knee in the dog's chest. (Even being a cop in NYC working on 42nd Street back in the day, this was one of the worst fights he'd ever been in.) After five minutes of holding the dog down while the dog struggled, it seemed to be slowly submitting. Slowly giving a little slack to the neck, the dog came at him again, and again the grappling when on. This would have been a great WWF cage match. Finally Vicious realized that this was not a fight he wanted to be a part of. Bill got up and dragged the dog into a sit. (I think the dog was more tired than Bill.) The next thing Bill observed was that Vicious was looking for affirmation from Bill. He could see it in Vicious' eyes. Bill petted the dog on the head and all Vicious wanted was to never go through that nightmare again. Bill never noticed the owner during the event but when it was all over, he looked at that 110-pound woman and said, just like Charlie Daniels says to the violin player on the commercial, "Here's the leash, ma'am, that's how it's done. Now you do that the next time he becomes aggressive." With tears in her eyes she said she couldn't. Bill said you have to find another home for Vicious.

Bill felt bad about the next thing he did but he told her that he was going to report the situation to the Police because the nine-year-old son was in danger.

With a dog like Vicious, Bill would not attempt to train it regardless who the owner was. There is no guarantee that an aggressive dog, regardless of how minor or severe it is, will stop that aggressive nature. I know a guy on TV says that any aggressive dog can be trained, but this is one of the few areas of training that I totally disagree with him.

Some aggressive dogs are not the result of the owner unless it has been abused. There is no cure for aggressive behavior and I challenge any Dog Trainer who would train an aggressive dog that will guarantee that it will never bite someone again. For someone to make such a guarantee would indicate that they are the biggest fool you will ever meet.

Another lady called Bill one day and wanted training for her husband's Pit Bull "Tippy" that bit her on the arm. Bill was recommended to her by her boss who had a Lab and had trained them a few months earlier. After getting some information from her, the lady said she was afraid of the dog. Well the dog sensed fear, and had no problem taking advantage of the situation. Since her husband had no interest in training the dog, any kind of training would be a waste of their money so Bill declined the opportunity, since everyone has to be on the same page when it comes to training. Bill actually advised them to find another home for Tippy since there was a fear issue and an uncooperative husband.

About four months went by and the lady in a pleading voice called again. She again asked if Bill would train her husband's Pit Bull. "What happened now?" was his first question. She said the dog bit her in the face and now she's "scared to death." Any sane person would be scared to death in that situation. Bill again asked if her husband would cooperate with a training program. She immediately said he would not. The husband said the problem had to do with her and not Tippy. I said that the best solution is to find another home for Tippy. She said that was not an option for her husband. That's a sad commentary on what we would call for lack of a better name a real "Bonehead." Bill then said unfortunately, it might be time to get rid of "Bonehead" since he obviously cares more about the dog than you.

Men, let's make this plain and simple. This is directed to all the Boneheads out there. If you have a dog in your home that shows any signs of aggression and you don't want to train it, man up and get rid of the hound. No one in any home should be fearful of a dog. (I know there are ladies that do not want to give up aggressive dogs also.) Get over the problems that you have created with your dog, find another home for it and move on with your life.

You might say that Police K-9 dogs are aggressive. Well that is true up to a point. The difference is that Police K-9s are trained to be aggressive, but only when they are required. That is only when a bad guy is resisting arrest, or when chasing a bad guy to apprehend him. (Women don't usually resist arrest or run because they don't want a bite mark on their skin.) When selecting a dog for the K-9 Unit, the training unit would not accept an openly aggressive dog. The dogs would be given an aggression test. If the dog was unnecessarily aggressive, it would be declined immediately. The important point concerning Police K-9s is the dogs are trained as to what circumstances they are to be aggressive, and there is a highly trained handler with them.

Every spring Bill and Jasper would do a presentation in Harlem, NYC, for children's day. They would do a practice apprehension. This is a staged K-9 apprehension with another handler who played the bag guy with a gun. They would show the kids how Police Dogs can take a bite out of crime.

Jasper would then demonstrate agility and go through an obstacle course using different things in the park such as benches, garbage cans, jumping over fences and whatever else there would be to entertain the kids. After the agility course Bill would walk Jasper into a crowd of kids and let them pet him. The situation was very controlled and Jasper was on leash all the time. That dog soaked up the attention of each kid. Later on, the same demonstration would be conducted for another group of kids.

This is **Bear** talking now and I have an interesting story to say about dogs and kids. Anyone who knows me knows that I wouldn't scratch myself if I thought I would hurt a flea. Anyway, I was playing with my cousin Gianna who at the time was 3½ years old. Gianna and I always have a great time together. She can lie all over me, pull my ears and she actually looks in my ear, (probably wondering if I have a brain). She can step on my tail, roll me over and as long as I'm with her, I'm in 7th Heaven. Remember I weigh 95 pounds. Gianna only weighed 35 pounds. One thing that I have always noticed when Gianna was playing with me is that Bill and Debbie never let us out of their sight. This is for good reason. They know that I would never intentionally bite my friend, but you can never predict the unpredictable. What if Gianna accidentally fell on my stomach and it hurt enough for me to react? I wouldn't be the same for the rest of my life if I reacted in a bad way and bit her. It really wouldn't have been my fault.

It is the responsibility of every dog owner to never let the dog out of sight when kids are present. Don't take a chance with a child.

I'm going to say it again; as good as your dog is, never leave it alone with a child under 10. Even if you think the child has enough responsibility to take care of the dog alone. If you are going to err, err on the side of caution.

Let's go to another story. One of the canines in the unit was home with his handler. During the night at about 3 am, the handler's wife got out of bed and walked towards the bedroom door. Unknown to her, Tass was lying on the floor and she accidentally stepped on his leg. Tass reacted and unfortunately planted four canines in her calf. He realized what happened right away and released but it was too late. Yep, you guessed right, four punctures. Who was at fault? The result of the very informal investigation was that the dog should not have been in the bedroom. Tass was never allowed in the bedroom but that night sneaked in after lights out. Precautions should have been taken.

Look, anything can happen with a dog. Hey we have teeth. In fact we have 42 of them of which the four canines in front are pretty big. Unfortunately the unexpected can happen. The situation with Tass was not because he was aggressive. What would you do if someone stepped on you when you were sleeping on the floor? You might not have bitten that person, but you would probably do something that wasn't pleasant. Always expect the unexpected, and never anticipate that because you have the "Perfect Dog," it will not misunderstand the circumstances of a situation.

In conclusion, aggressive dogs can be trained as long as all the people in the dog's environment are on the same page regarding the training. If a dog trainer says that they will guarantee that a dog will never bite again, go to the next trainer on the list. Get a trainer who will say that they can give you better control in the situation but not guarantee that it will never bite again.

Overweight Dogs

Well this is another situation where the owner must take responsibility. I am a five-year-old Lab named **Ollie.** I've been battling a weight problem most of my life. I only eat the food that is placed before me. My owners are responsible for what I eat. What's a dog supposed to do? Well because we don't know that we're over weight, we don't know there's a problem. Some people think it's cool to have a 125-pound dog. Very few dogs can handle that weight. If you know anything about Labs they will literally eat anything.

Solutions to overweight dogs are simple. Cut back on the food. You might say, "But the dog will be hungry." OK, it's time to use some "common sense." What would you do if you have a weight problem and wanted to do something about it? Probably go on a diet. Do the same for your dog. Put it on a weight control food plan and cut back on the amount you give it. If the dog is still hungry, supplement the food with canned vegetables such as carrots as an alternative to the shorted food. If the dog won't eat the carrots find a veggie that they will like. There are no calories or fat in this supplement. Baby carrots make a great snack for a dog. We love them and they are crunchy.

Don't forget that an overweight dog can get heart disease and other related illnesses just like humans. Hip problems with a large breed overweight dog can be a major problem.

Talk to your vet about other possible solutions.

A Dog Relieving Itself In The House
(A Story And A Solution)

When it comes to offensive behavior, any dog over four months should not be relieving itself in the house. Is this a problem with the dog? Well, it could be, but in most instances, it is the owner's fault for not taking the proper time to train it to relieve itself outside. This is **Kalib** speaking. Because I didn't like to walk on the leash, my owners did not like to take me for walks to relieve myself. We lived in an apartment which made things worse, because they couldn't just let me out the back door to the backyard. I was a hand full and felt that I could do anything I wanted. I was winning the battle. I had an occasional accident, which led to more frequent accidents. These accidents could have been avoided if a few simple things were done right from the start.

The first problem was that the area that I relieved myself in was never cleaned with a deodorizing and scent neutralizing cleaner. Dogs are driven by scent to relieve themselves. A male dog for example will relieve itself by urinating on any object it can find even if there's only one drop left. Hey, we have to let the other dogs know we are still around, so don't mess in my territory. We even like to pee as high as we can to let the other dogs know how big we are. The second problem was that I was never walked on a regular basis to get the hang of things. The only way we can learn how to do something is by doing it over and over again. Don't forget that you should take the paper towel that you cleaned up with outside, and place it where you want the dog to relieve itself.

Basically, I guess what I'm trying to say is that it's up to you as to whether or not we're going to make a mess in the house. With puppies it's understandable, but we do learn very well at an early age. Concerning punishment when a dog relieves itself in the house, well that is a debate that many trainers have wide differences of opinion on. Coming from a dog, take into consideration whether or not it was an accident or just laziness. The most severe punishment should be to put the leash on the Martingale collar and bring the dog to the offended area. When you get there, Rover will probably know what is going on. If Rover appears to know that he did something wrong, then you know the accident wasn't an accident, but was laziness. At that point you would say NO!! And give a tug on the leash. You will then walk him outside and let him know where his do-do is to be done. It's as simple as that. You can also say a strong NO! if the leash is not available. DO NOT HIT THE DOG. In any event, somehow let the dog know that the behavior is unacceptable.

Food Stealing is something that is easily controlled. Common sense really applies here and you have to be aware of everything you do in the kitchen. Remember we talked about how a dog's smell is so much greater than human's. Well, some dogs think that anything on a counter or a coffee table that has a nice smell to it has their name on it. Hey, the best of us have gone through this. We know that we are supposed to eat from a food bowl, but human food is very tempting. Training is the key to this issue.

As we said in the obedience chapter, the Sit Stay Command is the most important command for the dog to learn. While in the kitchen, find a location that you can make the dog sit-stay or down-stay so that it is out of the way. The problem is enforcement of the command. You're busy cooking and don't have time. Find time to do some training when you are not cooking. The second alternative is to put the dog in another room.

If the dog is walking by and sees a snack that doesn't belong to it and steals it, then a correction is in order. Practice with a set up situation. Place some food on the edge of the counter. While on leash have the dog sit-stay in front of the food and give it praise when the dog doesn't eat it. Give a swift correction if the dog tries to eat it. Use a small correction if the dog tries to smell it. (Food reward training does not work as well in this instance.)

After the sit-stay routine, then walk back and forth in front of the food and praise the dog when it doesn't eat the food. Do not let the dog smell the food or even look at it. If it does try to look at or smell the food, give a slight tug on the leash for reinforcement. This takes a lot of practice and due diligence. Practice this every day until the dog gets it right.

Probably the best thing to do is to be extremely aware of what you are doing in the kitchen and keep all food off the counter while you leave the room.

CHAPTER 7

Selecting A Dog Trainer

If you don't know something,
Know where to find out about it.

My name is Aster and I have been through a couple of training programs. I am a Boxer and weigh about 74 pounds. Yeah, I have some issues but most of them can be blamed on my owners. We'll discuss them later. Please, don't get me wrong, I have been through a couple training programs with three different trainers. Two of these training programs were with my owner and he seemed more confused than I was. The problem is that most people don't know a thing about dog training. Most dog training customers usually have a comment something like this, "I've had dogs all my life — I know a thing or two about dogs." This reminds me of *"Howe's Law,"* it goes like this, *"Every man has a scheme that will not work."* That is especially true with people who want to train their dog, not having any experience with dogs. Those people are unfortunately sad souls who as, "know it alls" will rarely solve their problems without blaming the problem on someone else or the dog.

In reality most people don't know that much about dogs, except that they have four legs, they are covered with hair and have a tail on one end and bark from the other end. Sorry to disappoint you folks, but the real problem is that you do not know what your dog is thinking? Your dog has a mind of its own and to understand it, takes years of being with dogs and being extremely observant of your dog. You have to understand your dog's body language and its "voice tone."

This is one of the most important aspects of dog training. You just don't learn this from owning a pet, unless you are a natural at it and have been a dog owner for a long time.

My first experience with a trainer was at one of those big "box stores" that give dog training, or so-called dog training lessons as part of their services. My owner thought that this was going to solve all my problems. Interestingly the problems got worse. You see, these stores run their program with good intentions. The problem is that good intentions don't always have good results. In a recent training publication, Bill observed an ad for one of those "box stores" looking for dog trainers. Unfortunately it said "Dog Trainers Wanted, No experience necessary." They sent the candidates to a two-week school to learn about dogs. Well, in a two-week school, you will learn something, but it will not be enough to compare with the experience of someone who has been through a Police K-9 Program or a 4-H Dog Training Program. Basically, all I did was socialize with other dogs in our group of eight dogs. I would recommend these training environments as a good place to get a puppy socialized with people and other dogs, and get them used to riding in a car to and from the store.

My second experience with a dog trainer was being sent to a boot camp. It wasn't a bad time for me, but I did have a little separation anxiety. Since the trainer was good with dogs, he made me feel a little better. I finished with top honors and my owner came to pick me up and was given a one-hour lesson on the things I learned to do. This experience cost about 900 buckaroos. The problem with this was that I had become very smart and my owner was still at his incapable level. Saying it simply, I was beginning high school and my owner was still in the first grade.

My third experience with training was with a highly qualified private trainer. This training was six lessons, with each lesson being ½ hour in length. I was trained in my own home, which made life a little easier. The best part about this was that the issues that I had in my home were addressed in my home. Everything was a firsthand experience to me. My owner was explained the training requirements in easy to understand language. My master and I became bonded and were best friends from then on. He understood me and I understood that he was my leader.

The guy that is helping us write this book had a conversation with a so-called trainer at one of these "box store training centers." It was very interesting. The person attempted to explain how they used "food as a reward system." (We'll discuss that later.) She further said that they "did not train problem dogs," "did not do advanced off leash training" and, "did not train unruly dogs." That leaves the owner with "sit," "down," "stay," and "come" for 115 bucks and no guarantees. What kind of a training facility is that? You get what you pay for which is not much. It turned out that what they didn't do was more than what they did do. The other problem with this scenario is that you have to progress at the level of the slowest dog owner in the group. That's right, the owners usually have more problems than the dogs in group sessions. Since there is no one-on-one training, the trainer must occupy their time with 8-10 people and their dogs.

When looking for a dog trainer, the first question you must ask yourself is, how much effort are you going to put into the training process? Fifteen minutes a day does not seem like much time, but for many people with busy lives, it's hard to fit in. You want to make a commitment to your dog first and then to yourself. There is an old saying that goes like this, *"Everyone gets the same 24 hours in a day — the difference is how you use it."* Take this from a hound that has been through three programs. The failure of a dog making it through a training program is usually not the fault of the dog. IT IS THE FAULT OF THE OWNER. The late Barbara Woodhouse, a highly regarded dog trainer who was from England wrote a fantastic book titled, "No Bad Dogs, Just Bad Owners." Nothing could be closer to the truth. If there is a problem in your home with your dog, it's your fault. If you have a problem in any environment with your dog, it's your fault. This book is not about sugar coating answers to make you feel good. The reality is that the dog is on one end of the leash and the problem or solution is on the other end. Don't make excuses. Do something about it. If the dog is a good dog then you can take credit for that. Granted there are dogs that are easy to train and then dogs that are more difficult to train. That's where you have to pay special attention to the "Selection of a Dog" section of this book in Chapter Two.

Unfortunately this is sometimes the situation in Police K-9 Units. We have seen good dogs ruined by poor handlers. Fortunately, most of these good dogs could follow instructions better than the handler and made the handler look halfway decent in their job. Then there have been difficult dogs with good handlers and the handler had to work extra hard to make up for the dog. But the result was a good K-9 Team. Then there were good dogs and good handlers. Those were the K-9 Teams that stood out and everybody could see that there was something special about them. There was something different about their communication process. It wasn't magic. It was hard work. This is the same hard work that you must do with your dog. You might say that K-9 Teams are so well behaved because of the hours and hours of training each day. Well I'll let you in on a secret. In Police K-9 Training, the dog and Police Officer actually spend about 45 minutes to an hour each day performing training tasks with their dog. The rest of the time is watching other dogs doing their work. Do you honestly think that a dog can perform a working or training function for eight hours? Be realistic, the dogs must take breaks especially in the summer. The canines do not work at every exercise at the same time. The only time all the dogs and handlers worked together was during obedience training. It also is dependent on how qualified the trainer leading the group is. A Police k-9 Training Group will usually consist of between 10 and 15 dogs. The amount of dogs will depend on how many assistants are available.

After asking yourself how involved you want to get, you must determine what method of training you want. Some methods of training that are available are "food reward," "clicker," "positive reinforcement," and "electronic collar." Each trainer will have their own method that they have learned from a mentor or training program. Unfortunately, there is no State or Federal Certification for dog training except for Police K-9. Most trainers who say they are certified pay to be a part of an organization and that organization gives them a piece of paper saying that they are a certified dog trainer. This is usually done via the internet. There are good trainers who are not law enforcement trained and there are certainly very good dog training organizations out there. I know of a few trainers that over the years have gained experience to become very good and successful at what they do. Interestingly enough, the best of these trainers have the same training method as Police K-9 Trainers.

Questions To Ask A Prospective Trainer

1). How long have you been training dogs? Get references on their training experience going back several years. Good trainers will keep records. Make sure that they are a mature person and didn't just start doing dog training since he just taught his own dog how to sit. Remember, anyone can say they are a Dog Trainer.

2). How many dogs like mine have you trained? Generally Labs, Goldens, German Shepherds, and Rottweilers, are the more common breeds. Don't be concerned if it's been a while since the prospective trainer has trained your obscure breed. Their method of training will be applied to your dog just like any other.

3). What do you offer in your training? It is important to know what you are getting for your money. Trainers should either have a brochure that they will send you or a website for you to look at.

4). Do you offer a guarantee? If a trainer does not offer a guarantee then find another trainer. The author of this book explains the answer to this question this way, "As long as you, the owner, does the required 15 minutes a day training with your dog, it can be guaranteed that your dog will be trained as expected. A good trainer will be able to get your dog to do everything required of it in the first lesson. They will demonstrate to the owner during any lesson that the dog is doing exactly what it is supposed to do. That does not mean that the owner will have an easy time. Occasionally, the owner might have a problem during their daily training session. This is OK. A good trainer will be available via, phone, text or email to help you out.

5). *Can I call you anytime for advice?* A dog trainer should be available anytime to answer questions that the customer has. Remember, the trainer is working for you and you deserve answers. You should have the trainer's cell phone and email. Remember, trainers can have busy schedules so they might be with another customer and not answer the phone immediately. (We hope that a trainer will not answer their phone during a training session. Bill leaves his phone in his truck during training.) Simply leave a message with the concern and wait for a return call. It shouldn't take long to receive an answer for your concern. Bill has found that text messaging is the easiest way to communicate with a client.

6). *What do you offer after the training is finished?* Reputable dog trainers will offer what is called a "Service Warrantee." This is a lifetime "Service Warrantee," that will provide his/her service to you if a problem arises after the training is complete. In most cases a phone call will solve the problem, but there are situations where a visit will be required. This visit should be at no cost.

7). *Get references!!!* Make sure that the trainer has done this before. There are a lot of people out there that claim to be the "cat's meow" (sorry to offend my fellow dogs) but can't teach an elephant to eat peanuts. A majority of Bill's training customers come from references of people he previously trained.

With all this said, and I know this section went a little long, **DO YOUR HOMEWORK!!!** That is emphasized because hiring a dog trainer is some of the most important money you will spend. Do it right the first time and never worry about it again.

One other thing — you get what you pay for!! A $100 Training Program will get you a $100 Training Program.

A qualified Dog Trainer should cost between $400-$900 for a six-lesson training program.

In Review

- Make sure you get a qualified trainer with references. Ask local pet stores, veterinarians, vet hospitals, (not veteran hospitals but veterinary hospitals) shelters etc, etc.

- Do your due diligence in training with your dog for at least 15 minutes a day at least five days of the week. Take Sunday off and go to Church.

- Be comfortable with the training method you choose.

- Don't blame a lack of progress on the dog. You are the one who will determine the progress of the training. I've never seen a dog that couldn't learn, but boy oh boy, some of the people coming through training programs are almost impossible.

- Don't blame the trainer. A good trainer will get the dog to do anything. It's up to you to get it done.

Here's one final comment about hiring a dog trainer. Dog trainers are not going to get rich in this line of work.

If you attend any type of school, the protocol is to pay the admission fee at the start of the first class. The funny thing about dog training is that there are those customers that feel that it's ok to say, "Can I pay you next week?" after the first lesson is finished. Yeah, for you it's OK to pay the guy next week, but for the trainer, I think they would like their money when it was agreed on. Tradition has it that those folks who have the means to have anything they want are most guilty of this. The folks that are scrapping enough money to make ends meet seem to always come up with the dough.

Just something to think about.

———————
———

CHAPTER **8**

Methods Of Training

H i folks, this is **Skipper** and I hope you have been enjoying the reading so far. I also hope you are not one of the ones, who have been insulted, but in the dog world, we don't really care if you were. You probably deserved it anyway.

Hey, I'm the dog that never had any training except for TLC. I am unusual since most dogs that turned out as good as me had been through a good training program with a trainer like Bill. Looking back at my life, now that I am where all dogs go when time comes to an end, I did have a somewhat neurotic problem when I got older. For some reason I had a problem with wood floors. Who knows why? Maybe it was the wood boat dock that kept moving whenever I was walking on. Hey I don't drink so that wasn't the problem. It was just one of those crazy things. Ok I'll admit I'm a little neurotic. I have been advised that there are training options for neurotic problems like I had.

Well after I arrived at my final destination in my after life, I was able to hash out with my fellow departed dogs different training programs. I got the nitty-gritty of what was going on in the dog training world. It's really interesting and you just might find it informative. Here goes my first official correspondence back to those I left behind. By the way, the training methods are not listed in order of preference. Remember, trainers have their own methods that work for them.

Food Reward

Food reward training has become a fast growing method of training, with what I would consider questionable results. The problem with this type of training is that when there is no food available, the dog will shut down from doing what it is supposed to do. You see we can smell a lot better than any human, and we know who has the food and who doesn't. This type of training has no consequence for bad behavior. The dog is enticed to stop bad behavior by luring it away from that behavior with food. The dog only earns a food reward for good activities and no negative consequence for bad activities. In speaking with a food reward trainer this person has had problems getting several dogs to heel (walk right next to you with the right shoulder of the dog next to your left leg). The end result was using a head harness along with the food.

You people will never know how aggravating that piece of equipment is, and I have heard that from the best of my friends. As I stated in the training equipment section, head harnesses are not training a dog. This is creating an annoying situation that only an inexperienced person would do. These are generally group lessons.

Food reward, if ever used, should be used at the early phase of training and then wean the dog off it.

Clicker Training

Clicker training uses a small hand held device that makes a clicking sound when you press a small piece of metal. The clicker is clicked when the dog does something good and then the dog receives a food reward. The trainer must be trained by an instructor who is an expert with clickers. This can be either a group or private lesson.

Electronic Collars

Electronic Collars also called E-collars have been around for quite awhile. When most people hear Electronic Collar, they think of it in a negative way. Actually it can be a positive training tool if used properly. This training method can be very effective if used by an experienced trainer. Electronic Collars do have a purpose and traditionally have been used with hunting dogs or dogs with problems. The trend is growing fast for many dog trainers with good results. The cost for the equipment can be more expensive than traditional training methods.

E-collars have a transmitter which is held by the handler and a receiver which is attached to the collar of the dog. Receivers usually come already attached to collars. There is a sound option and an adjustable electric shock option.

Unfortunately, people purchase these gadgets and expect them to work wonders. They know little about how to apply this method if they are not trained properly. One of my Belgium Malimaur friends is a very active dog. He is exactly what the breed is ... a bundle of energy. Well his owner was tired of all the activity and decided to try an E-collar without knowing anything about it. Not realizing the setting goes from low to high, he tried it accidentally on the high setting. Well not much more has to be said. *Bada Bing Bada Boom.* The next thing he saw was his poor dog doing a couple backwards summersaults and then landed on the owner who finally let go of the transmitter. You talk about a dog thinking he was going to doggie hell. What an unbelievable and unnecessary act of abuse, to say the least. Too bad they wouldn't allow these to be used during a terrorist interrogation, (not that us dogs would be against that). If a person feels that they should use an electronic collar on one of my friends, at least have the guts to put it around your own neck and let your dog hold the transmitter in its mouth. Then we'll see how fast you want to use it on your dog.

E-collars are a great tool for hunting dogs and as I said, are a great tool for those trainers who use this method of training. We know of a lot of trainers that are very good with these and have had a lot of success.

Doggie Boot Camp

Doggie Boot Camps are locations that an owner can send their dog to for training. The trainers in my experience are usually very good, but, when the dog graduates, it is usually smarter than the owner. These establishments are the most expensive forms of training and generally use positive praise reinforcement (see below). After the dog is trained, (which usually takes 4-6 weeks), the owner will pick their dog up and be given an hour or two of training on what the dog has learned. Hey, most of the dogs going through this are more experienced and a lot smarter than their master. The owner is usually more confused and has no clue on what to do with their dog after they return home. The downfall with this program is that when the owner is not a participant in the training, he cannot comprehend what to do when they get home.

Private Versus Group Lessons

As with anything you get what you pay for. Take my friend **Bear** for example. Being the handsome Yellow Lab that he was, his owner researched the breed and found a breeder that was top quality. He paid $1,500 and never regretted it. He could have paid $500 for a Lab that he knew nothing about.

In dog training the same applies — you get what you pay for. *Group lessons are less expensive, but your group will only progress as fast as the slowest person in the group.* Did you hear what I said? I will emphasize it again. The slowest person will slow the progress of the whole group. Any dog can be trained. Don't ever blame the lack of training progress on the dog. Take it from an expert; there are certainly some pretty dense people out there. Of course there are some dogs that are more difficult, but those dogs require a special owner and a special trainer.

Group Lessons can be a good process of learning. You will save money. A single trainer group should have no more than three students. That is, three dogs with their owners and the trainer. If the group has more than three students, there should be proportional assistants.

Private Lessons *will individualize the training to the personality of the dog* *as well as the owner.* A good trainer will communicate the training exercise to the owner who will then communicate the exercise to the dog. Having a trainer that will explain what the dog is thinking will be a great advantage to you. It is very important that you do your homework when hiring a private dog trainer. Private Lessons can be held in a training center or your home. Home training will be more expensive.

When starting a training program, remember that there will be some confusion with the dog as well as you. The environment will be different. In group training, the location will be different. In private in- home training, an extra element is introduced, the trainer, who is making the dog do things that they never did before. So be patient with yourself as well as your dog

Private In-Home Lessons

Private in home lessons have the advantage of working with your dog in a familiar environment. The problems or issues that your dog has can be addressed in the area that they exist. This training is the most expensive but you will get what you pay for if you select the right trainer. Trainers that perform this service will also spend a session in a dog park or strip mall to socialize the dog with new people and other distractions.

To select a trainer refer to Chapter Nine and find one that fits your needs. Also request from the trainer their experience in the problem area or areas that you want to address.

4-H Training, Dog Club, Volunteer Shelter Training

A great place to get quality training is with a number of volunteer organizations. This is a great experience for kids. They will work with other kids in training their dog and the mentors are usually very good. Determine first that the training given by the group is the method you desire and that the trainers are qualified.

These groups are run by very dedicated people and the experience will last with a kid for a lifetime. 4-H groups are probably the most popular group to learn dog training. The folks are outstanding and the kids love it.

Positive Reinforcement Training

Positive reinforcement training is a training that finally worked for a dog named **Buddy**. Basically it rewarded him with "Praise" when he did something right. This could be a pat on the head or a verbal "Good Boy." If needed the dog received a little correction when he did something wrong. Many new folks in the dog training business consider this method training "old school" and ineffective. Most trainers that adapt to this method of training would then ask this question, If this were so ineffective, why are so many of our students, graduates of the "box store dog training" (food reward) programs? Over the years people have been trying to re-invent the wheel concerning dog training. "Positive Praise Reinforcement" has been around since Egyptian times. Most of Bill's training customers have been through the "box store dog training" programs that used a food reward.

Positive reinforcement is the oldest form of training in the US. It has been around since WWI. Over the years, many great trainers have been adopting this form of training with great success. It is the same training used by today's military units as well as most Police K-9 Units. It would seem to me that these are the people that you want to follow.

Positive reinforcement utilizes voice tone as well as positive physical affirmation and physical correction when the dog misbehaves.

Positive affirmation is a good pat on the head or pat on the side of the dog along with a "Good Boy" in a high voice tone. A correction will be a tug on the leash that transfers to the dog making their neck slightly uncomfortable. Take it from Bear who had problems with other training methods, this was the only thing he listened to. A dog's neck is one of the strongest muscles in their body and knowing how this method was use by Police K-9 Units, you don't have anything to worry about. That's another good point, if Police K-9 Units were using this method, and their dogs are the best behaved of any dog we've seen, how bad can it be? Again, when you hear someone say *"They* say it is bad for the dog." Remember to ask them, who is "they?"

The equipment used in positive reinforcement training is a leash and usually a chain training collar better known as a choker or we recommend a "Martingale collar" as referred to in earlier chapters. To properly apply this training, it is highly recommended that you find a trainer that is fully competent and experienced with positive reinforcement training before you begin. Most people don't realize that a training collar can be put on wrong as discussed earlier. Yes, there is a correct way and a wrong way. An alternative to a choker is a "Martingale collar" which cannot be put on incorrectly and is somewhat more effective in several ways. Both the choker and the Martingale are great tools when used properly. This book is not intended to be a training book but an informative guide to training. In dog training, there needs to be an accountability factor. That accountability would come in the form of a trainer who will hold the owner accountable. If you are experienced enough the trainer will not be needed.

A good trainer will explain what is required from you. *The result of your experience will be determined by how much effort you put into it.* Your dog will not train itself. Your pet might be the smartest dog in the world, but without the proper guidance it just isn't going to happen.

Again when looking for a trainer, consider the methods of training and which one you feel would be the most productive for you. From a dog that has experienced a few trainers, save yourself some money and go directly to a positive praise reinforcement trainer. These are either group or private lessons.

Basic And Advanced Training

Basic training is exactly what it says. The basic commands of dog training will be "Sit," "Down," "Stay," "Come," and "Heel." Most trainers will include the word "No," but with the way things are going today, "political correctness" dictates to some trainers that there will be no negative commands, go figure. One of the hounds had three training programs under his belt, the word "No" was important for him to learn. We'll talk about commands later. (Some trainers use "Eh, Eh" instead of "NO." That only makes the trainer feel good because, the dog has absolutely no reasoning ability to differentiate between words. We only hear the sound that the word makes. Dogs don't have a vocabulary. They understand the sounds that the word makes.)

Basic Training is done on leash. And generally lasts for six lessons that are ½ hour each. Most trainers can get the dog to "Sit" in 15 minutes and "Down" during the first lesson. While doing this, the trainer is explaining to you what will be going on for the remaining training period. What to expect in training will be discussed in another section.

Advanced Training is geared more towards "off leash" work and will require the same amount of attention on your part. That means 15 minutes of practice a day. Don't expect your dog to be ready for advanced training if you are not ready. The trainer will decide when you are ready to proceed.

Again whenever you inquire about a training program, ask if there is a guarantee. Most good trainers will say that they can guarantee that they could train your dog in a short period of time. The problem with that statement is, it's another story for the owner to be able to do the same with their dog. Dog owners are at a disadvantage since they are learning just as the dog is. That is not the fault of the trainer. It takes more work to change the habits of the dog owner. Again, do your homework and research who you are taking your dog to.

Many dog trainers find that a person with no experience with dogs will have an easier time training the dog. They are soaking everything up and they will not have bad habits to overcome. One big thing is that they will not have the know-it-all attitude that so many former dog owners have.

There are several other methods of training that will be discussed in the chapter explaining different types of equipment so make sure to read that chapter because it also refers to head halters and pinch collars.

CHAPTER **9**

The
Language Of Dogs

W ell so far you have been learning from dogs in written word. That is not our usual form of communication.

Learning the language of any animal is more of an art than a science. Books have been written about the language of animals. Most animals have the same body language and voice tones used to communicate with. The problem with most dog owners is that everything about their dog looks and sounds the same. They can't see a play bow, which is when the dog leans forward with its front legs on the ground, or a curled tail which usually means caution. To be able to correctly read your dog's body language, you must spend a lot of time with us and document in your mind what we're doing in every situation.

As a Police K-9 I have seen new handlers screw up the most obvious indications that their dogs gave. I am **Tass** and am for the most part an unusual Police K-9. I say that because I am a mix of Husky and German Shepherd. I will talk about why I said that later.

Dogs as well as any animal, communicate in "Body Language," "Sound Tones" (growling, etc) and "Odor." A dogs "Body Language" can be visually observed by people. That is, if the person is experienced at observing body language in dogs. Sounds coming from a dog are heard by a person or another dog. Most people know the sound of an aggressive dog but few people know the difference of the numerous other tones that dogs have. Odor is an indicator that dogs communicate between themselves, but let's not worry about that now. You're not going to go around like we do and smell dog butts. At least I hope not.

This section will not be a detailed discussion on every aspect of a dogs "Body Language" or Sound Tones. We are here to let you know what to look for and listen to, to understand your dog better.

Let me say a few things about the "Body Language" of an animal. Being a Police K-9, I was always providing various forms of communication with my handler. My handler was a great cop but did lack the ability to read me as well as he should have. I could read him like a book though. He could read other dogs better than he could read me. That might sound weird to you but in most cases that is not unusual.

Did you ever hear of the saying, "He can't see the trees between the forest?" Sometimes we are too close to a situation to really see what's going on. One of our trainer's favorite phrases was, "Ray Charles could have seen that," when we were working on narcotic indications in practice situations. The problem with most handlers (police and civilian) is that when they are inexperienced in working with a dog they are literally standing too close to it to understand what it is telling you. As a Police K-9 Handler becomes experienced, they stand back about 10 feet and watch the dog work off leash. The officer is then able to see what we the dog is telling them. A quick turn of the head or a stutter step would indicate that there is contraband in the area.

Dogs communicate with each other and people. Tails wag in different ways. A high wagging tail means a fun type of excitement. A low still tail means the dog is being cautious. Sound tones are the same way. A bark and a growl mean different things, and a growl and a bark could have different levels of meaning. My friend Jasper, sounds like he almost talks to his handler. He's not quite barking or growling. It's sort of in between like an "Arrr, Arrr, Arr." Only the handler knew what Jasper was saying because of his experience.

To really understand what a dog is telling you, you must be with dogs on a constant basis, and watch them and listen to them. You must be aware of every environment you are in. Then you have to watch and listen to what they are telling you. There are books written just on this subject so one chapter on the subject will be hard to explain everything.

CHAPTER 10

Equipment For Dogs

*Each new invention is eventually replaced
by a newer invention*

I n an earlier chapter we discussed equipment that would be used in the training program presented in this book. We are going to reemphasize some of this information and add a little more. Hi folks, this is Spanky. I'm the Jack Russell Terrier, you read about earlier. We are a free-spirit breed and it might take a little ingenuity to keep us in control, as well as a lot of persistence. I spent most of my life around a Police K-9 Academy. I've seen all types of equipment, all of which were good as well as some in the civilian world which wasn't. I'm going to explain some other equipment in addition to what you read about earlier.

Training equipment has been around for thousands of years, and as time goes by, improvements are being made. Modern Dog Training is not all that modern unless it has an electronic element. You see, going back to early Egyptian times, there is evidence of domesticated dogs. We can tell they were trained by the hieroglyphics. Since then, training methods have been tweaked. Equipment has also been improved on. That being said, with modern technology and new materials becoming available, better equipment is being developed all the time.

There are also a lot of gimmicks out there that have absolutely no value to dog training so be careful how you spend your money. Beware of infomercials.

You're only going to waste a lot of money on things that might seem like a good idea, but you'll never use.

Someone who was known to be "Trainer of the Year" came up with a modified choker. In the opinion of this author, it was greatly flawed. Not getting into the flaws, the so called "Trainer of the Year" sold several of his products to customers at a Pet Expo. The folks then came to the booth where Bill was selling our products. The folks that just left "The Trainer of the Year" booth complained to Bill that the collar he just bought did not work. No wonder why — the collar was about six inches too large and as I said, there was a simple design flaw which if the trainer was really experienced, he would have seen it during the proto type stage. I explained this to the dog owner and said they should bring it back for the right size. The folks went back to the "Trainer of the Year" after purchasing the correctly sized Martingale collar from Bill but were told that all sales are final and wouldn't exchange it because the product was used. A sign of a quality product is when the manufacturer will stand behind whatever they are selling. That doesn't mean that if your dog chews a leash or collar that you deserve a free new one. In the case of our products, we let customers use our equipment prior to them purchasing it. This is to make sure they are completely satisfied. Satisfaction in a product is something that every dog owner should require when purchasing a product for their furry friend.

A side note about "The Trainer of the Year." As we said earlier, anyone can call themselves a dog trainer. In the case of this trainer, people had to call or write in to vote for him. He had a big platform and solicited a lot of votes and won the coveted title.

Leads

As a 6-year-old German Shepherd I am a good example of what it takes to be trained as a Police K-9. I am Buddy and the K-9 that had two dog handlers with the same Police Department. These handlers were completely different in their approach to training a dog.

My first handler gave me a lot of leash, meaning that he never kept me near him and I had enough freedom to feel like I was in control. On the other hand, my second handler was more experienced and learned very fast that a dog on a short leash is more easily controlled. He had total control of me by keeping me on a short leash which was usually two feet.

The lead is only an extension of the handler or in civilian terms, owner or master. What I mean by this is that the dog at the end of the leash will only be as good as the person at the other end of the leash.

There are several *different types of leashes* available to anyone who wants them. There are *grab leads* sometimes called highway or traffic leads. These are short leads ranging in length from 12 to 24 inches and used for total control of a dog in close quarters. Police officers like using these when working near roadways. The *general lead* is a leash that is from 3 to 6 feet and for everyday use by dog owners. These leads are usually nylon, but can occasionally be found in cotton. Cotton is the most comfortable fabric for a leash and will not burn your hand as the nylon will if the dog pulls. That's why so many K-9 Units use them. Leather leads are also very comfortable, but can be pricey.

Some pet owners prefer to use an extendable or retractable leash. This leash coils up into a case that you hold, and extracts to give the dog more freedom. We don't like them because you have no control with the dog since it is so far away from you. Some of these retractable leads have a warning on them saying, "Caution — Can Cause Amputation." Suppose your dog runs out and is 10 feet in front of you. The dog then runs back and it wraps around your finger by mistake. (Remember anything can happen and always plan for the worst case scenario and hope for the best.) After the thin rope wraps around your fingers, the dog sees a squirrel and runs off. Ouch!! That finger could become the dog's next snack if it cuts it off. There are also quite a few stories of the dog wrapping the leash around the walker's legs and then running off after see another dog. Ouch!! That's a rope burn that will hurt for quite a while.

Rubber Leads that stretch, as the dog pulls are somewhat new and were developed around 2005. This is another product that gives too much control to the dog. These come in either 1-, 3- or 5-foot lengths. The purposes of the rubber stretch leads are to soften the pulling on the owner's shoulder and arm. Is that really training your dog? We have never seen a legitimate trainer use these in a training situation.

A Training Lead is a leash that is anywhere's from 15 to 50 feet. These leads are used for distance training and are very helpful in training a dog in hand commands and training the dog to come from a distance. Training leads are usually 5/8" cotton material. Theultimateleash.com has them in 15 and 25 feet, in black, olive, blue and red.

A lead that is becoming very popular is a lead used by Police K-9 Units and is manufactured by Best Friend Marketing LLC. It is called *"The Ultimate Leash."* This leash has 11 uses and is very helpful for training as well as general use. The Ultimate Leash was originally developed in the 1960's by two experienced K-9 Handlers. Best Friend Marketing has tweaked it over the years and is available in either cotton or nylon fabric in 19 different colors and patterns, as well as leather.

This leash can be purchased on line at www.theultimateleash.com. It is highly recommended that you use a leash that will give you the most control of your dog. There are times that you want a short 12-inch lead and times when you prefer a six foot lead and sometimes a length in between. For general dog walking you want to have as much control of your dog as possible. If you let your dog walk in front of you, he feels that he is in control and thus the leader. The retractable leads and training leads are not recommended since they give the dog too much freedom. On top of that consider this, don't forget the warning included with some retractable leads that warn the buyer of the possibility of finger amputation.

The best possible choice for a leash is one that gives you control of the dog and at the same time gives the dog freedom when they need to relieve themselves. As a handler you want comfort. Cotton or leather are the choice of

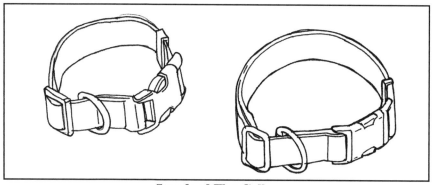

Standard Flat Collar

most handlers that know what they are doing. That is why many Police K-9 Units recommend it for their handlers.

Leather leads are very comfortable on your hand but again are also somewhat pricey.

Collars

Collars come in all different types and sizes. Each collar has a different use and there are arguments pro and con for each type. Being a professional Police K-9 I will explain and recommend the best ones to use.

The *Standard Flat Collar* is used by most dog owners. This collar offers no control and is a perfect collar for dogs that walk right next to their owner. It is also a collar that you can hang the dog's ID tags from. These collars come either in, plastic snap clips, metal snap clips or metal belt type buckles. For small very manageable dogs the plastic clips work well, but for the large dog and higher energy dogs the metal clip or buckle should always be used. Simply said the plastic has a better chance of breaking.

Training Collars or more commonly called the "choke collar" are very good for training only if the dog owner knows what they're doing. The problem is that most dog owners that use this collar don't size it or place it on the neck properly. On top of this they don't know how to use it. We recommend that a professional trainer explain the effective use of the "choker" before you use it.

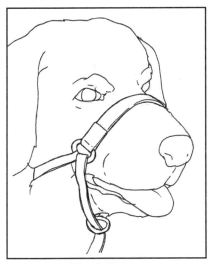

Head Halter

Choke collars have a disadvantage in that the owner must slide it over the dog's head. In doing so the collar is about two inches larger than the neck. Unless you keep the collar close to the top of the dog's neck, near its head, it loses its effectiveness.

Head Halters are used by many pet owners. They are also used by some trainers that have given up on the dog and want an easy way out to just walk the dog. A warning to people that use these collars is that they can cause neck injuries. The problem with head halters is that they are not training a dog but just controlling it. It is extremely uncomfortable for the dog. Many dogs will scratch at it or rub their snout on the ground to get it off. Sometimes there is even a fight to get it on. The dog basically cannot move its head unless the handler gives it some slack on the leash.

Picture yourself with a head halter on. Would you want someone controlling the movement of your head while walking with you?

Prong (Pinch) Collars serve a purpose to control a dog and make it

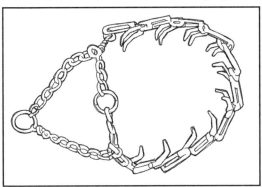

Prong Collar (Pinch)

uncomfortable when it pulls. When the dog is walking or behaving properly, his comfort level will be acceptable for him and won't even know it's on. Pinch collars should be recommended by a dog trainer for training purposes

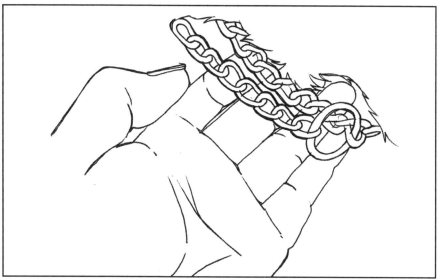

Martingale Collar (with four fingers between the neck and chain).

only. A pinch collar can be adopted with a choke collar or Martingale collar to transition the dog to the more traditional collar. This should be a last option for training. Pinch collars are good for small people with large, high energy dogs.

Martingale Collars are becoming more and more popular. This collar combines the standard flat collar with a training "choke" collar. Martingale collars come in a couple variations. Some are available that do not have a clip. With this type, you must slide it over the head of the dog and then adjust it to the proper neck size. To make sure it is not too tight you should be able to fit four fingers comfortably between the collar and the neck of the dog. Best Friend Marketing LLC, is now making available a Martingale collar that has a metal clip on it. This system makes it easier for the handler to adjust the collar while it's off the dog and when it is adjusted to the proper size, you just put it around the neck and secure the clip.

This collar can also be ordered through the Ultimate Leash website. These collars are available in matching colors to The Ultimate Leash.

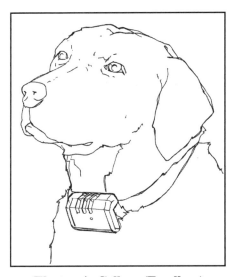

Electronic Collars (E-collars)

Electronic Collars are becoming more and more popular and do have a purpose, but users of these products should have the proper guidance when using them. Remember, that when you want to use an E-collar, try it on your arm first and see how it feels.

Bark Collars serve an important purpose, not so much for the dog, but to the people around it. All dogs bark. They communicate by barking. The problem is when the dog is in the backyard and decides to bark and doesn't want to stop then it becomes a nuisance. Some dog owners don't mind the barking, but the people around it should not have to tolerate it. That's why municipalities have barking ordinances.

A bark collar is similar to an electronic collar. There are several types but the most popular ones will give the dog an uncomfortable shock when it barks or it will emit a citronella spray that will become uncomfortable to the dog's nose. In the ideal world the dog will stop barking. We like the electronic collar better than the citronella collar. The problem with the citronella is that the dog can get used to the spray as time goes on. The E-collar has an adjustment on it to increase the shock if the dog keeps barking.

Miscellaneous Equipment

Crates are a great tool for dogs. Remember in an earlier section we discussed that dogs are cavernous animals. That means that they like to have an enclosed area that they feel protected to go to. A crate is a perfect solution to this. Crates are a great tool when you bring a new puppy into the house. Crate training is also used for house breaking the dog. Most dogs will not relieve themselves where they sleep.

The dog owner will have to be diligent when crate training. They will have to walk the dog every few hours to get the dog used to going in a designated place outside.

Unfortunately some dog owners don't pay enough attention when house breaking their dog and the dog soils the crate because it can't hold it any longer. A dog can get used to soiling the crate. This problem, that you the owner has caused, is sometimes very difficult to resolve.

Outside Kennels are a great way to house your dog when you do not have a fenced in yard. These are chain link fence sections and can be purchased at most large hardware stores. The standard size is around 4 feet wide and 10 feet long, and can be either 4 feet or 6 feet high depending on how big the dog is. With the fencing you will purchase hardware that holds the corners together. The best flooring is a solid concrete pad which will be easy for cleanup. Don't forget to wash the floor a couple times a week and rinse it thoroughly, to prevent the dog from getting a soap burn on its underside skin. If you have a dog that can potentially climb, get a roof.

A doghouse would be a good addition and can be placed outside with a hole cut through the fence. Just make sure you attach the house to the fence somehow. We are creative characters that can get out of almost any environment if you don't take precautions. The sun can be brutal on a dog so a plastic corrugated roof is recommended. These are better than tie outs since the dog knows its boundaries.

Tie Outs are a system that attaches to the ground and the dog is tied to it with a long wire. This is very frustrating to dogs because many times we cannot reason why we are tied up when there is plenty of ground all around us. Dogs tend to charge to the end of the wire causing it to become frustrated. There have been instances where dogs have accidentally strangled themselves by getting the wire wrapped around their necks. Of all the equipment on the market, this is probably the worst for the dog's quality of life. Many aggression issues begin with tie outs. Give the dog a break and don't frustrate it.

Life Jackets are important to have for your dog if going out on a boat. We can all swim. That's a given, but just like you, we can't swim forever. A dog can't reason enough where to swim and sometimes we can't even get up on a floating object. Err on the side of caution. Be prepared for the worst and always expect the best.

A *Dog Boat Ramp* can be very useful when taking a dog for a boat ride and it wants to take a little swim. For a short swim, take the life jacket off. The boat ramp simply attaches to the back of the boat and floats. The dog simply walks up the ramp onto the boat then shakes like the dickens and gives everyone a shower, whether you needed one or not.

Dog Air Conditioner Mats are great if you do not have central AC. Dogs for the most part like cool surfaces to lie on in the summer. The dog AC is a mat that circulates cool air through little holes in the mat, giving the dog an extra degree of comfort. (Remember dogs cool themselves with their mouths and noses. The only place we sweat is from our paws.)

Electronic Fences are a great tool for dogs that live in a yard that does not have boundaries. By that, I mean no fence or a separation between two areas. Dogs cannot reason where its boundaries are if they are not marked. Anything that separates two areas is a boundary line. For instance, a dog can be taught to stop at a curb so it doesn't go in a street. The curb is the boundary line. If you have a wooded area or a grassy area and you do not want the dog to proceed further than a certain point, then an electronic fence is a perfect solution.

An electric fence is a wire that is buried a couple inches below the surface of the ground. The dog wears an electronic collar that gives it a shock when it goes over that wire. Several feet from the wire the dog will hear a beeping come from the collar to warn it of where it is. Training is included with commercial units. You can get a low end unit and install it yourself.

A *Harness* is a piece of equipment that has limited success. People always tell us that they use a harness because it stops a dog from pulling. Maybe to some extent with a "no pull" harness that might be correct. The problem is that harnesses are placed over the shoulders of the dog which makes pulling very comfortable. Remember, if a dog is walking in front of you, it is the leader, not you.

In the dog world, harnesses are made for pulling. Sled dogs, competition pulling dogs, and tracking dogs use a harness because it is a motivator to pull. Another reason to use a harness is if the dog has a throat problem. Many dogs that have a short snout require a harness because their breathing can be impeded with a collar.

These are just a few products that might interest you. There are thousands of types of equipment on the market. Some are worthwhile to have. Many are someone's idea of how to reinvent a better mouse trap. Be cautious when buying a product especially from a TV pitch guy. Sure some of them are good but before you make any purchase other than the basic needs, do a little research to see if it will do what you expect. Also, do not buy something if you have an emotional attachment to it. Make sure you are making the purchase for logical reasons.

CHAPTER **11**

Training Your Dog
(More Words Of Wisdom)

There are no secrets to success,
Only hard work

O K, this section is going to be discussed with you by a couple hounds that know a little bit about dog training. Remember Jasper, he was a smart dog and had a handler who thought he was smart also. Little did they know that both had a lot to learn?

This book is not going to teach you the formal "Sit," "Down," "Stay" commands of training in detail. That should be left to a Dog Trainer. A trainer is the best source for you to learn about training your dog. Books are good for advice but a trainer can look on and take a personal approach to you and your dog. The trainer will observe your interaction with your dog and pass on comments that will benefit both of you. If you want to train yourself then your experience will most likely be failure. If you do have any success, it will take you five times as long to learn the system. Self training is good if you already have experience.

This is Jasper again. I'm the one who bit my handler twice because he thought he knew everything. What a laugh!!!

Most people that look at dog training, with the exception of a few, think that just because they had a dog when they were young, they are automatically qualified to be an expert on dog training. Nothing could be farther from the truth. I know this from experience. The family I had before I was dropped off at the K-9 Unit thought they knew everything, until I got too big for the house. Then it was off to the K-9 Academy, and the real fun started. It was an eye opening experience for me.

The basic notion of dog training is that the owner (and other members of the family) becomes the leader of the dog or better described as the pack. (Remember we discussed the Alpha dog earlier.) Now you must become the alpha leader of the pack

Training should be started the first day you bring your dog home and at a slow pace. You don't want to start a strong training program for obedience immediately. Instead, you do want to teach your dog where it should relieve itself so that it is not using your floors as a bathroom. Then teach it some basic manners regarding how it should behave in the house. Simply put, if you start early, you will cut your problems in the future. Training should be conducted daily, not as a job, and should be fun for both you and the dog. Too often, people bring a new dog into the house and expect too much from it. The dog doesn't know where it should relieve itself, nor does it know its boundaries. These are simple things that the owner already knows and has to convey that to the dog. Hey, we're not mind readers.

Training is nothing more than a matter of repetition, until you and your dog get it right. The training is for you, the owner, as much as it is for the dog.

It's Bathroom Time For Rover

The first thing when teaching your dog to relieve itself outside is to walk it to an area in the yard (or other specific location if you live in an apartment). Do not carry the dog to where it should relieve itself. I will admit that the smaller ones are cute and cuddly, but you are doing yourself no favor by carrying it. You're only spoiling it and the dog will expect you to carry it to its do-do area. Believe it or not, the four legs with paws that we have are for walking regardless of how big or small we are. I don't care how small your dog is, it can still walk. Find a specific location in the far side of your yard and bring it there and make that area the dog's permanent bathroom. Stay there until it relieves itself and then give it a great deal of excitable praise. Walk the dog inside and then immediately walk it back to the same location.

Sometimes dogs get lazy and want to relieve themselves inside. If you bring home a puppy, that's all they know. Relieving itself inside is what is done in a litter of dogs. It is best to get some type of marking system to place around the designated relieving area to show the dog where it is supposed to go. This takes work. It is best to pick up your dog early on a Saturday morning so you have the weekend to work on this. If the dog has an accident in the house, wipe it up with a paper towel and bring the paper towel to the designated area and leave it there. The dog will smell the area and know that the area is designated for relieving itself. When cleaning up the soiled area, make sure that you neutralize the area of odors. Do not use ammonia to clean the area.

Training should be an everyday activity that is not routine. Playtime should also be a daily activity. As a dog that has been through the program, and has probably done more than 99.99% of the dogs that have been on this great earth, I had to be reinforced with training on a daily basis. Our minds do not have the comprehension that a human does, at least most humans. Sure we can remember what we should do on a daily basis but if our handlers (owners) don't spend just a short period of maybe 10 minutes a day with us, after we complete training classes, your efforts in training will be a waste of time and good money. As a dog, I continually wanted to be the alpha leader of our little pack. If that issue was not addressed every day, I would have succeeded. My partner did obedience with me for 15 minutes every day for six years before I started to calm down enough to realize that I was in a losing battle. He was definately the leader of our pack. In my business of Police K-9, it was important for him to be the leader since I could easily have gotten into plenty of trouble if I were not totally obedient. New York City is a dangerous place for any dog. The daily training goes for every dog and every dog owner.

Many dog owners don't understand that to train a dog, you cannot apply an approach that would work with a human. *Dogs are animals and do not have the ability to reason.* By this I mean that we can't figure things out. Sure we can in some instances figure an easier way around an obstacle, or figure out how to get into a pantry door for food, but to do most things that our masters want, we must be trained. In applying this training you must show us how to do it. This is done with training tools. Leashes, collars, training leads, are some of the equipment that you would use.

Training requires that you be consistent 100% of the time. If you give a command, you better back it up and reinforce it if the dog disobeys. During basic obedience, do not attempt to give commands to your dog if you do not have it on the leash. If in the house, have the leash in your pocket or very close by. If the dog has a problem understanding what you are saying, simply put the leash on the collar and show it what needs to be done then give it some praise.

A common complaint of dog owners is that "my dog doesn't come when I call him." Well sir or ma'am, how much time did you spend teaching your dog to come? The same works with kids. If a child had no socialization for two years, would they know how to conduct themselves without being trained? *Dog Training takes time, patience and understanding.* A dog is a dog, and you can't expect much from it if they are not taught to do a task. If you're realistic about your expectations then your training experience will be a great success. Another requirement for dog training is to make the training period fun. Dogs can get bored and there is nothing worse than a dog that wants to lie down when you give the command to sit.

In the K-9 Unit, we would do our regular obedience training, and after a good performance I would receive a firm pat on the head along with excitable praise by rubbing my sides with both hands. My handler would say "Good Boy, Good Boy" with a high pitched voice. I knew I did a good job and the excitement from my partner, made me want more. Off we went to the next exercise.

Let me share an interesting story with you. My partner Bill and I were doing drug searches at a major urban transportation facility. Along with us were Federal Agents. I hit on (found) a shipment of narcotic contraband. For my positive indication on the package, he threw me a rolled up towel that had tape holding it together. I couldn't have been happier. He played tug of war with me, and boy I knew I did a good job. The Agent with us said to my Bill, *"Is that all you're going to do for your dog. Jasper just found a bunch of drugs. He at least deserves a steak."* My partner said it like it was, *"These dogs work for fun. Their reward is praise and playing tug of war. They live for that rolled up towel or in some cases a ball. Jasper might like a steak, but I can't carry a steak with me wherever we go."*

Just as I had something to look forward to, you must make sure that your dog has something to look forward to when it does a good job, and that doesn't mean food. Quality positive reinforcement is what we live for.

There is an interesting verse in the Bible that seems to be meant for dog owners. Gen. 1:28: *God blessed them (Adam and Eve) and said to them,"Be fruitful and increase in number, fill the earth, and subdue it. Rule over the fish of the sea, and the birds of the air and over every living creature that moves on the ground."* I don't want to preach to you but I don't see where it has any exception for dogs. You see dogs are creatures that move on this earth. The problem with many dog owners is that they don't want to be the rulers over their pets. They want to be friends with their dog, and don't want to do anything that would be a burden to their wonderful Fido. Hey we all agree that the dog and you should be best friends. The important thing is for you, the dog owner, to become the master. We need a leader, so why not it be you?

Many pet owners have a bad habit of loosing interest in training and then complain about the dog being stupid. Whose fault is it? They don't continue training after the training program ends and then the dog regresses. Whose fault is that? Any problem with your dog falls squarely on your shoulders. Maybe we will lose a few readers after this, but those people wouldn't get it anyway. Don't forget the Howard Huge cartoon. It's good to hear the story again. There is an old "Howard Huge" cartoon that explains this best. Howard Huge is lying on a couch. Two small boys are discussing Howard's activity or lack thereof. He obviously shouldn't have been where he was. The young boy who was the owner of Howard said to the other boy, *"I trained him, but he untrained himself."*

Training is a daily event. All it takes is a 10-minute effort, every day and your problems will be solved. This might sound simple, but, it really is. This works for any method of training. Make training a part of your routine and make it fun. Again, as Barbara Woodhouse would say, *"There are no bad dogs, only bad dog owners."* Get the training with a professional trainer and cut your losses and save the aggravation from trying to do it yourself. Then continue your training and work it for the rest of your dog's life.

Dog's are masters of "Body Language" and Voice Tone." In the animal world, pack animals (dogs are in that category), vie for dominance. In a puppy litter, the mother dog has no problem picking a pup up by the neck and making it do what she wants. Dogs understand a physical response is sometimes necessary. Of course you will never injure or hit your dog but positive praise reinforcement and a mild correction is what we understand. In the real world of animals, being uncomfortable is part of the learning process. In the wild, a dog would not be treated comfortably if he did something wrong in his pack. This is an instinctual understanding of how the pack mentality works.

It is not entirely understood why, but dogs are "Masters of Body Language" and "Voice Tone." By this, it is meant that they know and understand the feelings of people by sensing, odor, uneasy movement and differences in voice tone. Since dogs can't communicate by understanding human vocabulary or have the ability to speak, they must use their inherent senses. They can see in many ways better than us, and can definitely hear better than us. Dogs are colorblind and see shades of black and white. There are some studies that suggest that dogs can also see shades of blue. Dogs are near sighted and when in close proximity can pick up the slightest of movement. Sight hounds on the other hand can detect movements at greater distances. The hearing abilities of a dog are fine tuned and people don't realize how sensitive their hearing is.

The most advanced sense we have is smell. Dogs have an olfactory system that is much larger than yours. Yep, that means we can smell better than any human. Consider the size of our nose to you humans. They can sense things in humans through their olfactory system that you cannot imagine. We are onto you without you even being aware of it. As a Police K-9 who spent years sniffing out drugs, we were trained by our officers who would attempt to disguise the contraband with everything under the sun. Coffee, chlorine, grease, or anything you could think of and it wouldn't fool us. They would even shrink wrap things and place fabric softeners around it. Nothing worked. We could find everything we were trained to find. In the real world, outside the training setting, the bad guys did the same thing and didn't have a chance. The drug runners have tried it all so I'm not giving away any secrets. When they can change the smell of drugs and bomb materials, then it will be a different story.

My lesson here is that we are a lot more astute to your game than you are to ours. That is why you need a trainer that understands the personality traits of dogs. We can size up humans much better than most humans can size up us.

Now let me get to voice tone. If you ever listened to dogs playing, you would hear a growling higher pitched tone, which would be a play tone. As the play became more serious, the growling became deeper. The deeper the growl, the more alert the other dog must be. If the situation got more serious, the growling becomes very deep and in many cases, a fight would evolve.

With humans, your voice tone is extremely important. It is important that you communicate with your dog in low, medium and high tones depending on what you are communicating to your dog. On occasion, get down to his level and play with him so he understands that you're not this big towering creature always standing over him.

We already discussed this but this is a very important aspect of training that is worth repeating. Remember if something is repeated it should be taken very seriously. Voice tones are communicated in three levels:

1. A "High Pitched" tone will indicate praise. For a man this is more difficult because you have deeper voices. We understand men to be vocally more dominant than women. Women on the other hand have the higher pitched voice and have a natural praise tone. The problem with this is that when we hear a woman screaming like she has a "lit up firecracker" in her pants, we think that she is praising us, or is trying to play with us. When in fact she is ready to have a breakdown because of what we just did. Always take into consideration the situation and your voice tone when communicating with your dog.

2. A "Low Pitched" tone is the "I mean business" form of communication. This can be associated with a deep growling "NO!" Or "PHOOEY," or "DROP IT." The dog doesn't understand the word but will certainly understand the tone of your voice.

3. A "Medium Pitched" tone is used for giving commands. This is your normal voice tone. Sit, Down, Stay, Come and mid-range tones are those that the dog understands for commands. Praise or Correction tones are different. Lower your voice tones ladies when giving a correction.

Communication must be a work in progress until everyone in the household understands how to do it. One of the most difficult things for a dog to understand is mixed signals from several people in one household. If one person in the house is getting dog training then everyone should be getting the same training. It's not fair to the dog to receive different forms of communication from everyone in the house.

A dog can respond differently to the same voice command coming from two different people. Suppose the father says in a command (mid-range tone) "Sit," and the mom says the same command (high-range tone) "Sit," who is the dog more likely to listen to? This is where the mom is wondering why Rover doesn't listen to her and listens to her husband. Practice your voice tone. Men, you must practice, raising your voice to a higher pitch level to let your dog know that you are pleased with its performance.

Believe it or not, dogs don't have a vocabulary. I heard that from one of the dogs from the unit that went to Massachusetts with the family on vacation. Well the kids were quite confused since in New England, the alphabet does not include the letter "R." The kids didn't know what a "Ca" was. But the dog did when a New Englander said, "Get into the Ca." What the heck is a "ca?" the kids would ask. The New Englander might say things a little differently but we understand as long as the voice tone is correct, we will understand the meaning of what you want.

What Age Should I Train Our Dog?

At three months, a dog can accept basic command training. Sit, Down, Stay, Come, Heel are easy for the dog to comprehend. Don't forget, at three months a dog is equivalent to a two year old child. You cannot expect a two year old to comprehend much, so apply the same logic to your dog. You cannot expect a three month old dog to have an attention span of more than a minute or two at most.

Advanced training, which includes distance control, off leash commands, hand commands, and any other commands you might wish to train your dog, should only be attempted after the dog has mastered the basic commands and be started at a minimum of six to nine months, depending on its maturity. Your trainer can determine that.

As dogs grow older, they become a bit more independent. They become somewhat like teenagers and begin to have a mind of their own. If the dog has had training, and the dog starts to regress, start all over with the basic commands. Make your dog sit (on-leash) for 15 minutes. Let the dog know that you are taking back control, and there is no negotiating. Most good parents wouldn't let their kids get away with as much as they allow their dog, so why put up with the aggravation with your dog.

Whenever you start a training session it is good to exercise your dog prior and get some of their energy out of them. In the K-9 Unit, they found that a somewhat tired dog was a bit easier to handle than a dog with 100% energy. Don't forget, training should be fun and your voice tone and body language should indicate that you are excited to be with your dog and you mean business. Remember your attitude will trickle down the leash. To say it a little differently, your leash is like an electrical cord carrying energy to your dog. If you're plugged in, the dog will be plugged in.

How Long Should I Practice With My Dog Each Day?

Most dog owners have a hard time finding time to practice with their pets. As a dog we can feel this and it gets easy for us to regress when training exercises are not reinforced on a daily basis. For the most part, 15 minutes at day is sufficient for obedience training. The best way to do this is to break it up into three segments. Train five minutes in the morning, five minutes in the afternoon and five at night. This routine will let the dog know training is an ongoing experience that is a part of its daily routine.

Where Should I Practice?

Practice in different locations. That means in the house and outside the house. Practice on different surfaces. If your home has carpet, wood floors, tile floors, a concrete floor; and your outside has grass, concrete walkways, pavement driveway — you must practice on all of these surfaces. Our police dogs worked on black top and concrete. We were urban dogs, although most of us lived in the suburbs. There is grass in New York City, but sometimes it's hard to find.

Our training center was black top and concrete and the buildings had tile or concrete floors. We found that whenever a dog was on grass, they would act a little different. Some would attempt to run and act a little more playful. It didn't take much time to realize that since we were not doing training on grass we had to start just in case we ended up in a park for an assignment. The dogs who lived in the suburbs thought that grass was just for play time. The dogs that lived in the city had the hardest time since they didn't have the opportunity to be on grass that much.

Can I Practice Too Much?

As long as the practice is made to be fun for the dog, you can practice for extended periods of time. Try not to practice longer than 20 to 30 minutes at a time though. Dogs do not have a long attention span. Unfortunately, many dog owners have an even shorter attention span. Mix up your training and don't work on the same sit-stay for a long period of time. At the beginning, you will not have enough work to do for more than a couple of minutes. Wait until the dog is familiar with the ritual before you extend the sessions. Make sure that as your dog progresses, introduce new elements of training. Obstacles are a lot of fun for dogs to navigate. I loved the running jumps, climbing over walls or going through a tunnel or crawling under a park bench. After the basic obedience is completed use your imagination. Any object that will not create a hazard will be good for using on an obstacle course. Use your imagination to find ways to train your dog.

What If There Are Distractions?

Distractions such as cars, squirrels, other barking dogs, etc. should be avoided during the first couple of lessons. A distracted dog and owner will absorb a minimal amount of information. As the dog and owner progress in their training it is good to introduce common distractions so both of you will be comfortable with any situation. It is very important for the owner to read the dog's body language when in training. This will tell you when a distraction is approaching such as a squirrel or another dog. The dog will see, hear or smell the distraction long before you do.

CHAPTER 12

Train Your Dog
In Six Weeks

A true example of how to train your dog.

T his is **Bear** again. I am an eight year old, Golden Lab who is owned by the author of this book. I am a good example of how a dog should be trained. I came into mom and dad's house at four months old. When I was adopted they were very happy, because mom wanted a Golden Retriever and dad wanted a Yellow Lab. With me they got both. I am proud to say that I am a very well trained dog, but there are times when I need a little extra attention or reinforcement. That means I try to do things my way sometimes. If I didn't have these people as my masters, I would probably be out of control and on my way to becoming homeless. (Yikes, I never want to go through that again. Homeless and being a Retriever, how am I going to eat?) Every day they do some kind of training whether it is a sit-stay in the kitchen while mom is cooking dinner or down-stay when dad is watching a ball game on TV. You see, when you train a dog, you must make it a 100% commitment for the rest of your dog's life. Granted it does get easier but at first, it did take some work on their part. At the end of this chapter, you will find a weekly training schedule.

The first time I met mom and dad, they played with me and let me know that they liked me. That feeling was obvious. The other thing I noticed was that they knew a thing or two about dogs. Dad had very firm hands and a deep voice. It was obvious that he was going to have control over me. Mom on the other hand had soft hands and a higher voice. At first glance I immediately thought that she might be easy.

Mom and dad found me at a Pet Expo in Pennsylvania. A Golden Retriever Rescue had just accepted me from a rescue in Indiana. I was pretty shy in the new environment and felt lonely. Dad was the first to notice me. When he came to me he sat down on the floor. I felt pretty good about this, because everyone else was towering over me. Even though he was 6 feet 3 inches and weighed 210 pounds, I felt comfortable with him. Something about him told me that he was ok. What made him so interesting to me was that he took me and rolled me over on my back and held me there for a minute or two until I stopped moving. I never felt threatened by this but realized that this is what happened to me when I was with my real mother. I basically gave up and let him know that he was the one I would follow. After that he let me up and petted me and said in a higher pitched voice "Good Boy." Something like this happened to me when I was with my littermates and my real mother got mad at me. Only she was a little harder than he was. She held me by the neck and shook me and pushed me down. There was also a deeper growl when she did it. I wasn't abused by either of them, but I got the message. My real mother and new father meant business. That was the language I understood. They were in control and I had to listen.

For a dog that is a little more established in their lives, you might not want to do the same thing after entering a new home. Socialize with it at first and make the dog feel comfortable. Then after a half hour you lay the dog down and hold it there for a minute or two. To lay the dog down, you would put the leash and collar on the dog. That would be a Martingale collar or a training collar. Pull up with the leash using your right hand instructing the dog to "Sit" with the command tone. No one said this would be easy. Remember, training a dog is an art and not all people can accomplish this skill. The more techie you are, the less success you will have. A "brainiac" who lost their common sense in the 3rd year of college will be no match for a dog.

After getting the dog to sit, you would place your left hand on the shoulder, (not the neck), and push down saying in a command tone, "Down." If there is a little struggle push a little harder. Again, nobody said this would be easy. Sometimes, it might be easier for two people to work on this together. *DO NOT GET FRUSTRATED!!* You can also slip the front legs forward to make the dog a little off balance. This is always easier with a puppy and smaller dogs.

Mom came over to me a little later and approached me the same way dad did. She sat on the floor and did the same things but this time her touch was not so soft and her voice was noticeably deeper. This was kind of unnatural for me but did make an impact on me. After being on my back for a couple minutes, my new mom let me up and praised me in her normal voice, which was very soothing.

My first inclination of these two people was that they liked me and that they were not going to coddle me. Hey look, I'm a dog and not a baby. I don't need coddling — neither does any dog. If you want to ruin a dog then just spoil it with attention that you would give a child. All dogs of every size, (including the toy breeds) should be treated as dogs. No exceptions. This is not being mean spirited but is being a good dog owner. Dog problems exist because of bad owners who either: 1) don't have the time to take care of their dog; or 2) the owner thinks the dog is just like a human and will treat it that way. Humanizing a dog only creates confusion. Instinctually, the dog is confused about the situation and problems will result. Again as Barbara Woodhouse says, "There Are No Bad Dogs, Just Bad Dog Owners."

When I got to my new home, I thought it was pretty cool. Even though it was 10:30 at night, dad took me to a place in the back yard and waited until I did #1. When I did, he gave me some excited praise by saying, "Good Boy — Good Boy." I knew that I did something good and didn't even know what "Good Boy" meant. I knew by the sound of his voice he appreciated what I did. We went back into the house and then went right back out. This time I did #2. Again I was given a lot of excited praise and went back to the house. Then he took out a big box and put a towel on the floor of it. "Oh no," I thought I was going into solitary. The box was pretty big. Dad knew I would eventually grow into this thing that I would later know as "The Crate." He coaxed me into the box after I had a couple licks of water. A radio was turned on with a talk radio station and I went to sleep.

The next morning dad got up early and took me to the same spot and the same thing happened. I did #1 and he said "Good Boy." We went back to the house and right outside again. No #2 this time though. After going back into the house I was put back into the crate. The crate made me feel safe. In reality, we are "cavernous" animals and feel comfortable in a close safe surrounding. I found that my home was going to be the kitchen for one year with wooden gates on all the exits so I couldn't escape.

Even though I was four months old and old enough to begin training, they waited a couple of weeks to let me adjust to my new environment and get my confidence in them that they loved me.

After two weeks in my new home we began our training program. Training your dog for basic obedience should be an easy and fun task. Unfortunately, for most people it is not. If training were an easy task, everyone would have a perfectly obedient dog. Unfortunately, there are a few "wing nuts" out there that don't have all their screws torqued down tightly. Stop the havoc and give your dog the life it should have. This isn't a politically correct statement, but heavens forbid we just want a good life for your pets. *If you have a pet, (any kind) treat it like it is a valued treasure and you will have a friend forever.*

The following section is for those people that have a good handle on their dog already. By this I mean that their dog knows who the boss is, does not jump and doesn't persistently bother you when told not too. Remember, some dogs are easier to train than others. Remember **Spanky?** Well if you have a Jack Russell Terrier, which some people refer to as a Jack Russell Terrorist, you will have your hands full. Even the most experienced trainer realizes that they will be a challenge.

Six Week Training Schedule

Week 1: . . . . Sit, Down

Week 2: . . . . Sit, Down, Stay

Week 3: . . . . Sit, Down, Stay, Heel

Week 4: . . . . Sit, Down, Stay, Heel, Come

Week 5: . . . . Sit, Down, Stay, Heel, Come

Week 6: . . . . Sit, Down, Stay, Heel, Come, Hand Commands

This isn't rocket science folks. The key is to not over think the situation as a scientist would. It's a dog you're working with, not a fancy computer program. Use the most basic approach that you read about earlier. Spend 15 minutes a day in five minute increments. That's right five minutes in the morning, five in the afternoon, and five in the evening.

Do not proceed ahead of this schedule. Dogs can only comprehend so much, so stay with the program.

CHAPTER 13

Some People
Are Really Strange

Y ou read the title of this chapter correctly. Those of us who are canines can size up most people within a few seconds. The problem for owners is that we know you better than you know us.

This chapter could not have been thought of except for an email received by my owner one day. This is **Bear** talking. I'm the dog owned by the author of this book. I can be a blockhead and have received excellent training from a guy that has been around the dog-training block a few times.

One day he received an email from a dog owner that he trained six months prior. The dog was a Vizsla. Duke was exceptionally smart. Everything that he was supposed to do, he did with no problem on the first attempt. That is with his trainer, brother and the husband. Remember, good experienced dog trainers can train a dog in a couple of hours to do full obedience. That's because they are experienced and have had a tremendous amount of time working with dogs, reading their body language, and understanding the characteristics of the breed. Remember one other thing; a good dog trainer will not need food for rewards, head harnesses for control or any other extreme method etc., etc. All they will need is a training collar (the Martingale collar) and leash.

The email went something like this. "Bill, I need help. Duke keeps jumping and bothering me. I can't carry anything without him trying to grab it. I yell at him but it does no good."

This person received the same six private lessons as everyone else. Duke was a perfect gentleman when he completed the training. What went wrong??? As far as Duke was concerned, he was only doing what comes natural. He regressed because the follow-up training was non-existent. This will usually take place in about six months after training is completed if there is no follow-up training. Dog's for the most part, don't want to do anything but what we want to do. And if not kept in check, we will create mayhem. When we are trained, or should I say, when our owners are trained, they then train us. It is required that we receive reinforcement training on a regular basis after the training sessions end. That doesn't mean when the owner feels like it. Ideally, the training should be every day for a couple of minutes each day.

In the case of Duke, his follow-up training by his owner stopped when the last lesson ended. Duke's owner did email Bill for a couple of questions after the training, and did ask a question by phone, but the reinforcement never continued. Concerning the response to the bad behavior, I can never recall once, when Bill ever said that yelling at a dog was a good way to convey a message.

Yelling only raises your voice and a raised, higher pitched voice will only encourage the bad behavior. The dog thinks, in their mind, that they are being praised for the bad behavior. Yelling also lets the dog know your emotions are coming unhinged and it will certainly take advantage of the situation.

When Bill left his house to go on this follow-up session, he said to his wife, "I bet she isn't using the Martingale collar." His first observation at Duke's house for the follow-up was that Duke had a very nice leather collar on instead of the Martingale collar that he was trained with. The reinforcement with the leather collar could not work since it did not offer the same effect that the Martingale collar did.

It was obvious that the owner was more confused than Duke. After Bill arrived and the Martingale collar was put on, Duke became a different dog. The owner said Duke was being so well behaved because Bill was there. That is partially true. When Bill arrived, Duke was in the location where he was supposed to be, in the threshold area between the kitchen and foyer. He was excited to see his trainer. The difference was when Bill put the Martingale collar back on and a little tug was given Duke calmed down. Duke then remembered the reinforcement effect of the collar. The owner controlled Duke in a very acceptable manner after that session and hopefully life will be easier in their household only if the reinforcement efforts are taken. We have our doubts though.

The moral of this true little story is that training never stops. That goes for the owner as well as the dog. Being the blockheaded Golden Lab that I am, I need reinforcement on a daily basis. Sometimes I need it more than that. If I didn't get the reinforcement as I do, I would be an out of control animal that would be hated by my owner and anyone around me. The reason no one would want to be around me is that I would be acting like an idiot, but thanks to my owners, I am well behaved.

Let's rehash the best example of how things really work. This is so important to repeat. As I said in that Marmaduke cartoon, Marmaduke is laying on a couch obviously enjoying himself. Marmaduke's master, (a young kid) is standing next to the couch with another kid. His master then says to the other kid, "I trained him, but he untrained himself." I hate to keep saying it but *dogs do regress and it is the owner's responsibility to prevent it.*

Trained animals will regress from their training routines if not reinforced. This works for circus animals, zoo animals, Sea World animals, as well as Brody the Bear, a trained Grizzly Bear.

Dog owners cannot call themselves the "Master of their Pet" if in fact, do not have full control. In that case you are only a "dog owner." If you don't have total control of your dog, it is your fault, not the dogs. That is a choice you made. Being in control does not mean that you took your dog to training. The dog could be a perfect dog but you, being who you are, are far from the perfect dog owner. This has happened many times. If you have a trained dog and it doesn't listen, then blame yourself.

Another interesting observation about Duke's owner is that whenever Bill attempted to reinforce a command, the owner cringed and said, "Oh, poor Duke, I don't want to hurt him." She was training the dog with her heart instead of using her head. She knew that there was nothing done to Duke that would hurt him. A quality dog trainer will do nothing to hurt a dog. That means the dog will not be physically hurt nor will the spirit of the dog be broken by any kind of behavior. Duke's owner should have purchased a lap dog instead. Whenever you train a dog with your heart instead of your brain, you will lose. "Good Luck." After this session was completed, Duke's father, Pat and brother Mike did a wonderful job with him.

Fast forward six months. We received a call from Duke's mother. All Bill could think of was. "Oh brother what now?" She was so excited and said that she needed help in training her new Boxer puppy. Just what she needed, another high energy dog in the house. Bill was truthfully honest with her and simply said that you had a hard enough time controlling Duke, How are you going to control two of them? She didn't have an answer and guess what? Bill refused to train her with her new dog. Sometimes it's impossible for dog trainers to save dog owners from themselves.

The husband wanted the Vizsla, which was the wrong dog for the household since it would be crated all day. The son wanted the Boxer and mom and dad gave in. And mom, well she just accepted the dogs even though she didn't want either. Unfortunately the dogs knew that she couldn't handle them. The dogs treated her accordingly. The moral of this story is: if everyone is not on the same page when bringing a dog into the house; give up on the notion that you will have a happy family.

Folks, if you have any doubt about selecting a dog, do some research and contact a qualified trainer and get their opinion, then use them for the training that the dog will need.

CHAPTER **14**

Some Dogs
Seem To Have The Idiot Gene

H ello. This is **Bear** again, and I have to admit that I have a pretty good life. In fact, I have a great life. I am well trained and can do almost anything the first time I am shown. I sit until my master says get up. I understand hand commands. I fetch the paper in the morning, and understand the body language and voice tone of every person I come in contact with.

I love life and there are no boundaries to what I think I can do. My master or should I say masters are Bill and Debbie. You read about them before. Bill is the guy who wrote this book. He's on top of every situation with me BUT sometimes wonders if I have a brain in my cute head. I like to test him once in a while. This is no different than what any other dog owner has to go through with their dog. The difference is that Bill is a professional dog trainer and understands that this is the nature of the beast. Most dog owners do not understand this.

Granted, I know what the consequences are going to be when something bad happens and I get caught. I'll try to do something just in case I get lucky and get away with it. For me it's worth the chance. Being a Golden Lab I have traits that are hunter in nature. That means, for lack of a better term, if I were a human, I would probably be diagnosed with Hyper Active ADD. I can say this because Bill had ADD growing up and just like me he tested every issue that came before him.

Dogs by nature are all different in their traits. Breed categories have different traits. Dogs within each breed can have different temperaments and traits. Dogs within each litter will have different temperaments and traits. There are no exceptions. You would think everyone would know this. You would also think that before they started a life with the furry hound they brought home, they would have researched the traits of their dog.

Let's get back to the idiot gene. Have you ever heard the term, "It's a dogs life?" What is meant by that is that dogs don't have a care in the world. For the most part, as long as we have food and shelter we are happy. No worries, no troubles, just let us do what we want. There is one problem with that scenario; *we can't always do what we want!!!* As pets, we have to do what our masters want. Case closed. The less a dog owner knows about their dog the more they think that the *dog* is an idiot. The truth of the matter is that the less an owner knows about their dog, the more of an idiot the *owner* is.

Not to be bias, but dogs are some of the greatest creatures that God created.

Dog owners cannot call themselves the "Master of their Pet" if in fact, they are not in full control of their beloved Fido. You are only a good "dog owner" if you don't have control. To become a dog's master is to have full control of your pet. Just because you have a dog and feed it, doesn't mean you know what you should about it.

In most cases, a dog's characteristics and traits are normal for what it is supposed to do. Every dog has a purpose and or a job. Suppose you have a Lab or a Vizsla like Duke and it's running all over the house driving the family crazy. Hey in defense of my buddies out there, the real problem is that you are not giving your dog a job to do and it's getting into trouble. Sure there is the exception like a Lab that just lies around or a Jack Russell that sleeps all day, but they are very rare.

So when your dog is driving you crazy and you don't know what to do, put yourself in the dog's head and think about how it feels. Do something positive. If your dog is so high energy you can do something very important, play fetch so it can release some of that energy. You can also take it for a long walk. This will release its energy and is a great stress reliever for you.

Do these two things and you will learn how much fun it will be to have your dog around: 1). Give your dog a job that it is supposed to do; and, 2). Get it obedience training. This will take your relationship to another level. You will appreciate your dog more and it will keep you as a friend forever. Take a look at what you're not doing before you complain about your dog.

CHAPTER 15

Common Hazards
To Dogs

I am Harley and have a few issues that involve curiosity. Over my lifetime, I have been to the hospital four times because I smelt an odor and felt that I should investigate. After investigating it I decided that I should do a taste test. Well needless to say, I need to learn a few lessons. Unfortunately, my owner needs to learn a few lessons as well. If they understood my olfactory system when I was at an early age, I wouldn't have gotten myself into trouble. They would have saved a lot of money and I wouldn't have been on my deathbed on two occasions.

Hazards come in many different variables. A car can be a hazard. Certain human foods (chocolate) can be a hazard. Certain plants can be a hazard. As a dog owner, you must be the one that watch for these hazards. Dogs, especially like me can't look out for ourselves. As I said in a previous section, "We can't reason." If something smells good then it must be edible.

Basic common sense applies to most situations. The exception is when it comes to food. Most owners realize that chocolate is not good for a dog. Dark chocolate is most dangerous because it can give an unbelievable buzz to their central nervous system. Fatty foods are not good because it can cause problems with an inflamed pancreas. If your dog has a painful stomach and is not acting normal get the pooch to the vet ASAP. Grapes and raisins can cause havoc on a dog's kidneys. These foods could be fatal if eaten in large quantities. Remember that smaller dogs will need less consumption than a larger dog. Another problem that could be potentially fatal to a dog is being overweight. Just like humans, overweight dogs are a problem and we can contract the same diseases as humans. To check to see if your dog is overweight the general rule is if you can't feel their ribs they are overweight. Look down at your dog while they are standing, if you can't see a taper at their waist, (just in front of their rear legs) they are overweight. Some people think it's funny to see a dog that is drunk. Well it might be humorous, but any owner that would do that to their pet is actually abusing it. Alcohol in any quantity could be dangerous to a dog. Don't be a jerk.

Food bones can be a problem with dogs, especially chicken, turkey, or bones from any other fowl. Don't even give your dog a steak bone. Any bone can splinter and become lodged in the throat, or digestive system. All it's going to do is cost you a lot of money.

So much talk about foods. There are other hazards in house holds that you would think are obvious. Cleaning agents and anything that you wouldn't eat yourself, keep away from your dog. If you lock the cabinets from your kids, do the same for your dog. We can be pretty creative when it comes to opening closets to get to a nice odor. Use child proof locks on your cabinets if you have an inquisitive dog. Hey, we have claws and can learn to open doors.

Certain plants can also wreak havoc on a dog. Mistletoe, poinsettias, and holly are Christmas decorations that are poisons to a dog. These are a list of plants that are hazardous to dogs: azalea, wisteria, laurel, rhododendron, rhubarb leaves, castor beans, lily of the valley, hemlock, locoweed, jimson weed, arrow grass, foliage of cherry trees, peach tree leaves and elderberry leaves. It is your responsibility to check out your home and determine if you have any of these plants around.

Antifreeze is probably one of the best known poisons for an animal. Unfortunately people think that the only place to get this poison is in the garage.

Never let a dog lick anything off the street or driveway because it might contain antifreeze. Antifreeze has a sweet taste and is deadly. Newer antifreeze formulas have a bitter taste to discourage dogs from licking it.

Driving with your dog's face out the car window is a hazard. That's not because we are concerned that you'll take a corner to sharp and hit a telephone pole either. Hey, the breeze feels great and the breath of speeding fresh air can be exhilarating. The problem is that in the spring, summer and fall, there are things called bugs that fly around. Yeah, just take a look at your windshield and you can see hundreds of the little dead critters splattered all over the place. Guess what, there are the lucky ones that fly right by and unless you have goggles over your dog's eyes, a major eye injury could occur. The next thing you know is that your dog is scratching its eye and you're wondering what is in there, forgetting all about the trip the both of you took to the store. There are dog goggles on the market, so if your dog wants to be a side ornament, at least protect its eyes.

Every potential hazard that we described (and there are more) can be a potential injury to your dog. Use common sense. If you wouldn't eat it, then why would you let your dog eat it? We can't over emphasize this enough. We smell some very appealing odors and they also taste pretty good. We don't know what's good for us or what's not good for us. You the owner must be our guardians.

CHAPTER 16

Dog Owner Etiquette

D og owner etiquette is one of those things that many dog owners cannot understand and many simply don't care about. Etiquette is required of the owner to make sure their dog is not offending or bothering someone, or disrespecting someone else's property.

Simply put, unless a dog is trained and conditioned to respect other people and property, it will not know what to do. "Hey," this is Kizzy talking. My owners never had a dog before and believe me they needed a way to control me in every environment.

You see, as dogs we don't know boundaries and we don't know if something we might do is offensive to someone. We are instinctual creatures. Jumping, peeing, barking and running are all natural things that we do. Hey for all I know your leg with pants on looks like a tree and when a dogs gotta go, a dogs gotta go. Yep, you've got a wet leg and it's not because I'm attracted to you.

This section is for those dog owners that are good to their dogs, but have not become the master of it. Knowing how to control your dog around people and other people's property hopefully will become a reality after reading this. "Respect for people and property is one of the foundations that our great country was founded on."

Dogs Bothering People

One of the most annoying things for invited guests is to have a dog jumping at you and trying to get you to pet it. Well that's natural for dogs to do. It's up to the owner to train the dog to "sit-stay" until the invited guests want to pet the dog. Don't forget one thing — maybe your guests don't like dogs and don't want to be bothered by them. (You invited the folks over. If they don't like dogs and you can't control YOUR hound then put it in another room and close the door.) This is why we told you earlier that the commands "sit-stay" is the most important command for a dog to learn. Again, teach your dog to sit and stay in one part of the room until you release the dog from that position. Don't offend your guests with an annoying dog.

You remember Bear, the dog that Bill owns. Well, Bear loves attention and will do anything to get it. Whenever company comes to Bill's house, Bear is commanded to sit and stay in the kitchen. Case closed.

One of Bill's friends once said that if he believed in reincarnation, the last thing he would want is to come back to earth as is Bill's dog. You see, Bear is extremely well trained and everyone can see that all he wants is attention. That's his nature. Bill is on him like "white on rice." Bear knows that he doesn't deserve that attention from a guest unless he earns it and his master gives the ok for him to greet people. As well trained as Bear is, he is sometimes just put in another room until he calms down.

One of the best ways to keep a dog from bothering company is to have everyone simply ignore it. The dog will soon realize that it is not wanted in the particular area and will find somewhere else to go. That means no physical contact and especially no eye contact.

Dogs Relieving Themselves
On Someone Eles's Property

Hey folks this is on you. *Never allow your dog to go on someone else's property unless invited.* You might say that the dog is only peeing and you can't see it. Well you will see it in a few days when the grass dies. The dog's urine actually turns to an ammonia-like substance and kills the grass. Any dog owner who allows their dog to walk on a neighbor's property has no respect for those people. You will soon be the talk of the neighborhood and be resented by every neighbor you thought was your friend.

If you are a homeowner and have a problem with dog walkers, kindly ask them to stop. If the action of your neighbor doesn't stop, then report it to the authorities and file a complaint. Make sure you document your actions and even photograph the offense. This might sound petty, but it is your property and you deserve respect. Don't forget that it's not the dog's fault. It's the owner's fault.

Excessive Barking

Ok folks, believe it or not, dogs bark. That's how we communicate. Now let's get something straight about barking dogs. As dogs we cannot reason and don't understand that no one else wants to hear about all our problems. Folks that allow their dogs to continually bark for periods of longer than five minutes are offending their neighbors. Many towns have "No Bark" ordinances that are usually during nighttime hours.

Unfortunately, many dog owners get used to the barking of their dogs and almost hear it as "white noise." "White noise" is noise that is there, but you get used to it and eventually don't even hear it. Hey, nobody should put up with a neighbor's barking dog unless it is alerting you about an intruder. If your dog barks more than it should, (5 minutes or more) bring it into the house and try to figure out what it wants. If you can't bring it in the house, then get a no bark collar and control it that way.

Suppose you have two dogs living next to each other. Yeah, we do communicate and sometimes bark to talk to each other. But for the "love of Pete," please don't disrupt the peace and quiet of the neighborhood. Use your brain and separate the hounds to opposite sides of the yard.

Dogs Running At Large

I love to run and sometimes that gets me into a little trouble. I guess it's probably a lot of trouble. When I get out of the yard, and have a little freedom, it just feels plain old good. What can I say, we're supposed to run. It's exercise and we need that. The problem is that when we intrude on other people's property, and possibly take a necessary #2, well that's my owner's problem and not the property owner's problem. It's offensive to the property owner and should have been prevented.

Preventing a runaway dog is fairly simple. You just have to have your thinking cap on and do a couple things. The first is a tough one: 1). Always keep your gates and fences closed (Duhhh — this ain't rocket science); and, 2). If you see that your dog has gotten out of your yard, do not chase it. It will only run from you. To get your dog back, try a couple things that might work. (These are not guarantees but try them anyway.) 1). Run in the opposite direction, it might follow you; 2). Get down on your knee and coax it back; or 3). Bring a treat out and coax it back. Don't forget, that if your dog comes back to you cannot correct it. It did come to you and that was the command you gave. You must praise it.

For the most part dogs that run usually will return home after a little while. They will not return if they know that you are angry, so keep your cool. Do not raise your voice — just call the dog in a calm manner.

CHAPTER 17

Dogs With Disabilities

H ello folk's this is **Zack** talking about this interesting subject. I am a four-year old German Shepherd Police K-9. Unfortunately, for some of my buddies, there are dogs that have disabilities. The shame about this is that they are sometimes discarded by their owners who do not realize that they make great pets.

Dogs can get along just fine with three legs, one eye, being blind, or being deaf. (And please don't name a dog with these disabilities "Lucky," because in most cases they don't know the difference. This is their norm.). The consideration here is that just because of a disability, it doesn't mean that they can't live a productive life. These situations do not require euthanasia. The pets might require a little more care but they can manage just fine. Just don't rearrange the furniture with a blind dog in the house. If you have a pet with a disability or know of anyone that does, you can go on-line and find support groups that will assist you with this situation. These groups can be can be of great help in your time of frustration.

CHAPTER 18

Dealing With
A Sick Dog

Sick dogs can cause quite a bit of stress for any dog owner. This is Jasper again. As I said I had a great life. Unfortunately, dogs do not live as long as their human companions. Old age usually sets in at around nine years. The larger the dog the earlier old age sets in. On average, dogs live between eight to12 years.

In my case, I retired from the K-9 Unit when I was 11. I was slowing up and wasn't as productive as I should have been. I was retired and replaced with another K-9 whose handler retired and didn't want to keep his dog. What a shame. When I was 13, I came down with a kidney problem where I could not hold my urine. Medication wasn't helping and I would just stand there and relieve myself. Bill could see in my eyes that I knew that I shouldn't be doing this but I could not stop and felt bad about it. He knew exactly how I felt. I was confined to the garage and kitchen for obvious reasons. After a year the condition became worse and my quality of life became difficult. I was becoming dirty and smelly. It was hard on me and the family.

There are some decisions that are very difficult and one of the hardest is what to do with a terminally sick dog. Here are a few things to consider when you have any sick pet:

1). Quality of life is essential for any dog and family. The problem with humans is that humans look at a sick dog and don't know what they are feeling. Sure the dog might be laying there and appear somewhat comfortable. This is where you have to know the body language of your dog and understand what it is telling you. Usually the eyes and ears are most revealing. I was very uncomfortable and everyone knew that it was time.

2). This is a touchy issue but as a pet owner, you should determine how much the cost of treatment for the dog will be. There has to be a limit. I heard of someone who said that they had become best friends with their veterinarian. When asked why, the person said that they spent $35,000 on their two terminally ill dogs to keep them alive for an extra year. I have one question about that. What was the quality of life for the dogs? Hey if you have that kind of money, I guess it's ok, but all things considered, is it worth the stress (for you and the dog) when the inevitable is obvious?

3). Are you keeping your pet alive for your sake or the pet's sake? Emotional attachment is something that is different for every person. Some people can separate themselves from a situation faster than others. Some people feel guilt when they have to make a decision about their pet. These are normal feelings. When you are not sure about how to handle a sick pet, ask your veterinarian what he thinks the pet is feeling. Do not ask the vet what to do. That is not a fair question. You can ask the vet if they can help you with the decision. When you have no idea what to do, say a prayer and ask God to help you with the decision. God has a way of giving comfort when these things get tough.

CHAPTER **19**

Loss Of A Dog

T his is a tough subject, especially for a dog to talk about. I am **Buddy**, a 90-pound, 6-year-old, German Shepherd and was the replacement K-9 for Bill, the author of this book. Bill took me from another handler that had retired. You read about me earlier. Yeah I'm the block headed German Shepherd. The original handler could have kept me but he was moving to Florida, and didn't want me anymore. Bill's original canine was K-9 Jasper (Badge #K9-7). They had worked together for 12 years and made almost 500 arrests. That's a long time for a police dog to work. It was obvious that Jasper was getting a little slow. Jasper also had a possible medical condition coming on. Long story short, I became the new K-9 while Jasper retired and relaxed at home. This was hard for everyone involved. Jasper had to stay home while we went to work. This was something that was hard for him to understand. This was hard for me, because I had to be transitioned with a new handler and this guy Bill was a no-nonsense guy when he was working. I had to perform 100% or he would train me until I did what he required. I fell into line pretty quick because doing what I was supposed to do was the easier path to take. We had a great career and became very active in making arrests and seizing narcotics. One thing I didn't do was work undercover as a Seeing Eye Dog with a blind man. Jasper was the master of that gig.

After two years, it was obvious that Jasper was coming to the end of his life. He still had his mental faculties though, but was being overtaken by a kidney disease. He still got excited at the sound of our truck coming around the corner and greeted us every day when we got home. As time went on Jasper was not able to hold his urine and was staying in the garage, where accidents could happen and not do any damage. As we said before in another chapter, you could look at Jasper whenever he had an accident and see in his face that he knew he did something wrong. Whenever this happened, Bill would walk over to him and say in comforting words, "It's okay boy, I know you can't help it," and then gave Jasper a good pat on the head and rubbed his sides. Jasper perked up and it was obvious that he felt better. You see, dogs might not be able to reason, but they do have feelings. Believe it or not, you can actually make a dog feel emotionally better. In every situation, please don't destroy the spirit or damage the feelings of your dog. They are forgiving and have an unconditional love that you, as humans will never understand. For some dogs those feelings will be a lick on the hand or they might rub you with their head.

Bill saw the end coming for Jasper, and talked about the situation with his mentor Dennis at the K-9 Training Center. Sometimes as a dog owner, you can't always look at this type of situation with an open mind. Bill's mentor said it was time, but to make it easier he said, "Why don't you let another handler take him to the vet for his final breath." That was agreed on and they decided that Jasper would be brought to the next in-service training.

Two weeks came by too fast. We were all feeling a little down. The night before my partner gave Jasper a nice steak. This was the first human food that Jasper ate while being with his partner. It was quite obvious that he enjoyed it. Jasper was one of the best dogs ever to be in Law Enforcement and deserved a very fine final meal. His dedication to his Police Department was higher than most of the police officers. His performance was above outstanding and his scent abilities for sniffing out narcotics were second to none.

Well it was time to bring Jasper to the K-9 center. Bill put me in the truck first. I stayed in a kennel in the back of the pickup whenever we went to work. Next it was Jaspers time to go in. You could see that Jasper was getting excited about going to work. Bill had to pick him up and placed him in the back of the truck, and immediately he began to run around like he used to knowing he was going to work.

On the way to the training center, Bill had a million things going through his mind. "Am I doing the right thing?" "Am I doing this too soon?" "What am I going to do when Jasper is not home to greet me?" We continued on our way. It was a long 45-minute trip for us, but not for Jasper. Jasper didn't know what was happening. He just thought he was going back to work. Feelings can get to the best of us. Bill was a guy that took no nonsense when making an arrest or if dealing with a bad guy, but when it came to having compassion for his dogs, he was the first to step up. Knowing he was going to lose the partner he had for 12 years is very difficult to say the least. Most people cannot comprehend what it's like to work with a dog, then return home with that same dog and it becomes a part of the family. Even the toughest person will experience a loss. It is said that President George Bush Sr. cried when his dog died. The story goes on to say that he didn't shed a tear at his mother's passing.

When we finally arrived at the training center, Bill left us in the truck and had a talk with Dennis. Dennis was very familiar with these situations and said that this activity by Jasper was normal and will be very short lived. They set some drugs out for Jasper to find in the warehouse of the training center. Jasper was going to have his final fun. They hid marijuana, cocaine, methamphetamine, and heroin. Marijuana should be easy to find as well as meth., cocaine a little harder and heroin would be the hardest to find.

Bill took Jasper out of the truck. It was obvious to everyone that Jasper was the only one that mattered now. Bill walked Jasper into the center and everyone greeted him and he became even more excited seeing people and other dogs he hadn't seen for a while. He remembered everyone. In the warehouse, Jasper was given his last narcotic search command to "Find Fetch." He was released off leash and did his normal search. It's hard to explain, but he had no problem finding everything that was hidden. He was a little slower though. Remember he hadn't done a narcotic search in over two years

Now things got even dicier. Jasper was like a new dog now, but Dennis reiterated that it was only a short-lived excitement, and Jasper's time had come. Letting go of Jasper was Bill's last act of love for his dog. Another handler took Jasper to the vet after a very warm and sad goodbye from his partner. He was cremated, and in a month his ashes were home with the family.

Prior to this happening, Bill had planned a vacation for the next week. This was probably the best thing that could have happened. He and his wife, who were equally attached to Jasper, as well as their two children, took a one-week vacation. Thoughts of Jasper were still on their minds, but this was a time that they could grieve and still have a good time.

After having the ashes for a couple months, it was decided that something had to be done with them. Bill remembered that whenever they went to their lake house in Pennsylvania, Jasper would run around the back of the pickup truck, when they were about 10 minutes away. Somehow he knew he was close to the place where he loved to run in the woods. Jaspers ritual was to jump out of the truck, and run around the property and come and sit next to the truck. Bill felt that the ashes were doing no good in a metal can so he took the ashes and sprinkled them on the same route Jasper took at the lake house. This has been the only sentimental thing that Bill has ever done.

This was Bill's closure to the loss of one of his best friends.

The purpose of this story is to express a few points. We all love our pets. Some people love their pets even more than their spouses. After meeting their spouses, it's no wonder why. Ask the guy that helped us write this book. He sees it all the time with his customers. Our pets are special to us but we must also realize that they are on this earth for a shorter period of time than we are. As we have said a few times in this book, they also cannot rationalize situations. They do not fear death. When our pets get on in age, they know that their time has come and in some instances are trying to tell us. Some dogs will even dig a hole to lie in, some will show obvious signs of illness, and some will just not want to be bothered with anything.

The following section is for those that are having a difficult time making a decision to in regards to their terminally ill pet. Please consider this and then say a prayer of comfort that God will help you. Your friend will finally be at peace and you will have memories to last a lifetime.

- At what point do you as a pet owner let go?
- At what point do you have to say that the quality of life or lack thereof, is abusive to the friend you have had for so long?
- At what point do you realize that it is more about the loss that you will go through, than the condition of the pet?
- At what point do you say you have spent enough money on your pet and realize that the quality of life has been horrible for both you, your pet and everyone around.

The passing of a pet is always hard. For some it is harder than for others. (Unfortunately, some people have a very cold approach to their pet and just treat it like a piece of furniture. That is unfortunate and we pets, pity that person). This is not to sound cold, but I want you to think about something. Your pet will come to the end of its life sooner or later. (We dogs don't have a 75 to 90 year life expectancy. Eight to12 years is our average.)

Should your family and friends have to go through a prolonged hard time, just because you want to keep your dog around for a little longer? We're not trying to sound mean spirited, but take this into consideration.

Do you know how your dog feels, even when it's on medication? The obvious answer is no. Your vet will in most instances say that your pet is comfortable. What does that mean?

Your vet is an important part of this process. Consult him or her, but don't ask them what they would do. It's not a fair question. Ask them the important questions such as: How is the pet feeling? How long does he have with, or without treatment? These are questions that the vet can't answer in exact terms though.

We are not proponents of euthanasia to dogs for no good reason and it is unfortunate that so many dogs in shelters must be put down because of over population. The problem is that we prolong the pet's life, not realizing that their quality of life is horrible. Euthanasia is a quiet and easy end to a difficult time in the dog's life. This is a very difficult subject to read about. Bill and his wife has been through this a couple of times and they can only offer the approach they took. Your potential loss is a very sad time in your life, and we are truly sorry for it. For those who have dogs whether ill or not, remember that the time will come when hard decisions will have to be made. These can be the hardest decisions you will ever have to make. Make sure that every day you spend with your dog is a quality day to insure that you have no regrets after the dog is gone.

For those that would like to make a personal statement to their dog I would recommend that you read this and write it with your dog's name. This was originally written in 1940 by Eugene O'Neil entitled **"The Last Will And Testament Of Silverdene Emblem O'Neil."** Jasper's and his friend's names have been included.

I, Jasper, because of the burden of my illness and realizing the end of my life is near, do hereby bury my last will and testament in the mind of my Master. He will not know it is there until after I am dead. Then, remembering me in his loneliness, he will suddenly know of this testament, and I ask him then to inscribe it as a memorial to me.

I have little in the way of material things. Dogs are wiser than men. They do not set store upon things. They do not waste their days hoarding property. They do not ruin their sleep worrying about how to keep the objects they have. They have no objects to bequeath except their love and faith. These I leave to all those that loved me. To my Master, who I know will mourn me the most, to my companions, Buddy, Olive, Spanky, Klause, Bear, Oscar and Zack and _____, but, if I should list all of those who loved me, it would force my Master to write a book. Perhaps it is vain in me to boast when I am so near to death, which returns all beasts and vanities to dust, but I have always been an extremely exceptional dog.

I ask my Master to remember me always but not to grieve for me too long. In my life I have tried to be a comfort to him in time of sorrow and a reason for added joy and happiness. It is painful for me to think that even in death I should cause him pain. Let him remember that, while no dog ever had a happier life, I have grown ill and pained. I should not want my pride to sink to a bewildered humiliation. It is time to say "good-bye." It will be sorrow to leave him but not a sorrow to die. Dogs do not fear death as man does. We accept it as part of life, not something alien and terrible, which destroys life. What will come of me after death? Who knows! I would like to believe that I will be in a place where one is always young; where I will someday be joined by companions I have known in life; where I will romp in lovely fields with those that have gone before me; where every hour is a mealtime; where in long evenings there are fireplaces with logs forever burning, and one curls himself up and remembers the old brave days of earth, and the love of one's Master.

There is much to expect, but peace, peace at last is certain; and a long rest for those weakened limbs and eternal sleep, after all is best.

One last request I earnestly make. I ask him, for love of me, to have another. It would be a poor tribute to my memory never to have another dog. What I would like to feel is that, having once had me; he cannot live without a dog! I have never had a narrow spirit. I have always held that most dogs are good (and two cats: Sam and Thomas). Some dogs are better than others — like me — and so I suggest a German Shepherd as my successor. He can hardly be as well bred or as well mannered or as distinguished and handsome as I, but my Master must not ask for the impossible. He will do his best, I am sure, and even his inevitable defects will keep my memory green. To him I bequeath my collar and leash and my heavy winter parka, which was made to order. I leave him my place in the car, which I loved so much and wish for him long rides with windows open.

One last farewell, Dear Master. Whenever you think of me, say to yourself with regret, but also with happiness in your heart at the remembrance of my happy life with you: He is the one who loved me and whom I loved. No matter how deep my sleep, I shall hear you, and all the power of death can't keep my spirit from wagging my wonderful tail.

Your life with your dog is special, and it should never be forgotten. A loss that you have had or going to have will be difficult, but, please consider this testament as an example for you to follow.

———————

CHAPTER 20

Types Of
Reference Material

A ster speaking here. Being a Boxer and weighing in at 95 pounds can prove very challenging for a dog owner. My owners, Christian and Jennifer, owned a Boxer prior to me coming along, but Casey (the prior dog) and I were as different as oil and water. Well I have to tell you that it was quite an experience for everyone involved.

When most people bring a new dog into their home for the first time, things can go either of two ways. The best possible scenario is for the experience to be positive, with a few wrinkles along the way, or it can be a disaster. In my case, I had a tough act to follow. Casey was also a Boxer and a great dog. I considered myself a great dog too, but Christian and Jennifer thought differently, because I was not the fast learner that Casey was, nor was I the mild mannered complacent hound that they had before.

Christian and Jennifer thought that all Boxers would be like Casey. It is guaranteed that each dog you own during your lifetime will be different in many ways. What do you do if you are suddenly in a situation that does not appear normal? The first and foremost is to find reference material that will help you in the area or areas of need. We also recommend that you find reference material for the particular breed dog that you have. If you have a mutt, then determine what breed fits closest to your dog and research that breed. The purpose in learning about the breed of your pet is to determine the characteristics of your dog and work with those instincts instead of against them.

An example of a bad case scenario is a kid goes to the local pet shop in search of a new companion. The first dog he or she sees is a Beagle. Mom and dad also fall in love with this newfound friend who will soon become "the dog from @#%&." No one in the house can figure why this beast will not listen. They don't know how a small dog can be so stubborn, or why they constantly have their nose to the floor or ground when you want him to do something. Think, for a minute about what just happened. First, those good-hearted folks bought the little puppy on impulse. Second, they knew nothing about the breed. Beagles are a wonderful breed of dog, with one problem — they are overly cute and have the attention span of a peanut when it comes to general obedience training. The other thing is that they are ground scent hunting dogs and are going to have their nose to the ground smelling the latest scent that went by. Yo, knuckleheads, that's what Beagles are supposed to do. They don't know how to do anything else except smell for critters on the ground and chase them. So now mom and dad who DIDN'T DO THEIR HOMEWORK are stuck with the little hound that should be with an owner that understands it. It's very frustrating, being a dog and seeing how badly people can screw up with our friends.

Research material can come in many forms:

Training Books: This Training Book is one form of material that will help you with training and understanding your dog. Books can come in many sizes and topics. I recommend that you go to your public library and find which book suits you best, and then purchase it at the bookstore or on-line if you can't find it. We recommend that you purchase the book to have for quick reference. It is also recommended that you keep notes of various events that come up during your dog's life.

As mentioned earlier, if you talk to ten dog trainers, each will have their own method of training a dog. Thus, each trainer has a training method that works best for him or her. Remember, modern day dog trainers did not invent the basic elements of dog training. Each trainer has learned or hopefully learned the art of dog training through a lot of hands on experience and by having an experienced mentor, although not all of them are what they say they are. We learned from Jasper, that there was someone who called himself a Police K-9 Trainer, when he was never even a Police K-9 Handler. The state requirements are that he had to be a handler for at least three years. That person gave himself a title and the police brass bought into it. Unfortunately, he couldn't teach a chimpanzee to eat a banana. Take a look at the trainer before you buy into his or her training method. There are plenty of great trainers out in the world of dogs and plenty that only give themselves a title.

Breed Books: The breed book will give you a detailed account of everything you need to know about the breed you are researching. The authors are experts in the breed and know what they are talking about.

Magazines: Monthly or bi-monthly publications are a terrific source of information. Some magazines provide a service to all breeds with a featured breed each month, while some are breed specific. Go to the newsstand and find which magazine will fit your needs. Most magazines address problem solving, training, products, first aid breeders and numerous other features, each issue.

Club Publications: Here you will find information on breed specific topics. You will also find local dog clubs and dog owners who would be willing to help you with questions on your breed.

On-line: The internet is probably the most advanced source of information available. Don't hesitate to use this invaluable source. Find a good search engine, and keep typing topics until you find what you want. **Ask.com** is a good place to start. Just type in your question and a source for your answer will follow.

Dog Encyclopedias: These are great sources of information. You will usually get a brief history of how dogs evolved from wolves, jackals and foxes. Now we can go from a ten-pound **Sheba Inus,** up to a 225-pound **Mastiff**. Encyclopedias also have a one-page reference to each dog breed, broken down by breeds traits, sociability, and training abilities. Basic training is also briefly addressed. We have several encyclopedias on hand and find that each one is well worth having.

Medical Reference Books: Highly qualified and dedicated professionals author these books. You will find some very good books on basic treatment you can give your pet at home. These books will also show you how to evaluate medical situations that might arise. Every dog owner should have a medical reference book on hand. We recommend that you don't let it collect dust. Take it off the shelf once in a while and browse through it so you will know what is there if you ever need it. KEEP IT IN A HANDY PLACE!!!!

CHAPTER **21**

Recording
Your Dog's Information

R ecording your dog's information is always a good idea. Suppose you were on vacation and had someone dog sitting for Rover? Would they know who your vet is, just in case there was an emergency? Do they know what medication it takes? You should keep on hand as much information as possible. This is good reference information for you also.

You want to have on hand your veterinarian's information. Have the name, address and phone number of an Emergency Vet Center available. It would also be a good idea to have directions on hand. These facilities are great places to know about since they are only open during times when your veterinarian's office is closed.

The following page is useful to record your dog's information. Please fill it out and let your family members and dog sitters that it is located in this book. If you have more than one dog, please make a copy and keep it this book for quick reference.

My Dog's Information Form

My Dog's Name:
_____

Date of Birth: _____ Breed: _____

Owner's Name: _____

Address: _____

_____

Phone: _____ Cell Phone: _____

Veterinarian: _____

Address: _____

_____

Phone: _____

Contact Person: _____

Emergency Vet Center: _____

Address: _____

_____

Phone: _____

My Dog's Medical Condition(s): _____

Medications: _____

_____

Endword

H ey folks this is Bill Lynch now and I would like to thank you for reading this book. Hopefully you found it entertaining and informative. This project could have never been completed without the help of the dogs and their owners that told their stories.

Over the years I had worked with so many people who are great dog owners. Unfortunately, I have found a few that were not. Anyone can be a dog owner but not everyone can be a dog owner that is the Master of their pet.

The deciding factor on how your relationship with your dog is depends on you. Almost every dog wants to be in a great relationship. That is their nature. Unfortunately, some dogs have been victimized by unfortunate circumstances that create behavior problems. Sometimes these problems can be resolved and some cannot.

As a dog owner, you must always understand the nature of your furry friend and accept that they are not human even though it appears that way. Remember that you have to use your brain instead of your heart to train your dog.

Well until I decide to do another project, keep working and loving your dog and you will be blessed for the rest of your lives.

Happy Woofing to all of you.

Police Officer Bill Lynch and K-9 Jasper working undercover as a blind man with his seeing-eye dog.

Police Officer Bill Lynch and K-9 Buddy at Kennedy Airport, NY, on narcotic enforcement duty.

K-9 Buddy conducting a practice apprehension on Police Officer Eddie McQuade who pretended he was resisting arrest.

Police Officer Bill Lynch and K-9 Jasper providing security at the World Trade Center bombing in 1993.

About The Author

Bill Lynch has been working with and training dogs since 1984 when he was one of the original six K-9 Handlers with the NY/NJ Port Authority Police K-9 Unit.

His Police Dogs K-9 Jasper and K-9 Buddy were involved in hundreds of criminal arrests, the seizure of thousands of pounds of narcotics and over a million dollars in currency. Bill and Jasper were the first K-9 team to respond to the 1993 WTC terrorist bombing, and perfected working undercover as a seeing eye dog and blind man in mid town Manhattan. Bill and his K-9 partners have worked with the FBI, DEA, Postal Inspectors, US Customs, Federal Bureau of Corrections, State, Local, and County law enforcement agencies.

As a Police Officer, he also worked undercover in drug buys. He worked in the Emergency Service Unit while serving in the K-9 Unit as a joint assignment.

In 1993 Bill founded Best Friend K-9 Training. After working over 26,000 hours with Police K-9s, Bill decided to retire and expand his business. He and his wife Debbie also manufacture "The Ultimate Leash" a leash with 11 uses, as well as Martingale collars, standard collars and other training related equipment.

Please visit our website: **www.theultimateleash.com** to find out more about our products and our love of dogs.

INDEX OF INTERESTING TOPICS

Please have your child/children
fill out the contract
on the next page,
and frame or hang !

Contract Between Kids And Their Parents

This is a Contract to have_____ in our house.
(Dog's Name)

I _____, accept the responsibility of
(Child's Name)
having a dog as my pet.

I will walk _____ in the morning, afternoon and evening.
(Dog's Name)

I will care for _____ by feeding him/her at the
(Dog's Name)
scheduled time.

I will spend 15 minutes a day playing and training _____.
(Dog's Name)
This can be at 3 sessions for 5 minutes each.

(Morning, after school and after dinner.)

I understand that _____ is my responsibility and
(Dog's Name)
I do not expect Mom or Dad to do my job.

If Mom or Dad are the one's taking care of _____
(Dog's Name)

it is their choice to either keep _____ in our home
(Dog's Name)
or they can find a new home for him/her.

Child's Name:_____

Mom and Dad's Name: _____

Date:_____

Parents, please stay consistent with your children.
This will teach them a lesson that will last for a life time.

For more information visit:
www.TheUltimateLeash.com

Contract Between Kids And Their Parents

This is a Contract to have_____ in our house.
(Dog's Name)

I _____, accept the responsibility of
(Child's Name)
having a dog as my pet.

I will walk _____ in the morning, afternoon and evening.
(Dog's Name)

I will care for _____ by feeding him/her at the
(Dog's Name)
scheduled time.

I will spend 15 minutes a day playing and training _____.
(Dog's Name)
This can be at 3 sessions for 5 minutes each.

(Morning, after school and after dinner.)

I understand that _____ is my responsibility and
(Dog's Name)
I do not expect Mom or Dad to do my job.

If Mom or Dad are the one's taking care of _____
(Dog's Name)

it is their choice to either keep _____ in our home
(Dog's Name)
or they can find a new home for him/her.

Child's Name:_____

Mom and Dad's Name: _____

Date:_____

Parents, please stay consistent with your children.
This will teach them a lesson that will last for a life time.

For more information visit:
www.TheUltimateLeash.com